CREATING
MIXED MODEL
VALUE STREAMS

CREATING MIXED MODEL VALUE STREAMS

Practical Lean Techniques for Building to Demand

Kevin J. Duggan

Foreword by Jeffrey K. Liker

PRODUCTIVITY PRESS
NEW YORK, NEW YORK

Most Productivity Press books are available at quantity discounts when purchased in bulk. For more information contact our Customer Service Department (800-394-6868). Address all other inquiries to:

Productivity Press
444 Park Avenue South, Suite 604
New York, NY 10016
United States of America
Telephone: 212-686-5900
Fax: 212-686-5411
E-mail: info@productivityinc.com

Cover design by Gary Ragaglia
Page design and composition by William H. Brunson, Typography Services
Printed and bound by Malloy Lithographing in the United States of America

Library of Congress Cataloging-in-Publication Data

Duggan, Kevin J.
    Creating mixed model value streams : practical lean techniques for building to demand / by Kevin J. Duggan.
        p.   cm.
    ISBN 1-56327-280-6
    1. Production management.   I. Title.
    TS155 .D75   2002
    658.5—dc21

                                              2002012393

06 05   5 4

In almost every book I have read,
there is an acknowledgment to the author's family
for their support during the writing. For the first time, I am the author.
I now know why such acknowledgments exist.

To my wife Christine, my guiding light,
and my children, Rebecca, Kevin, and Elizabeth.
This book would not have been possible without you.

Contents

Foreword

The Toyota Production System is elegant in its simplicity, yet complex when you consider all the aspects of this system of production. It is easy to understand the general concepts, and once the system is set up, each "associate" has a clear understanding of his or her roles and responsibilities. Simple visual management techniques help ensure each person will know what to do in every conceivable situation. Yet, managers and engineers are often perplexed when it comes to designing and setting up their own lean systems.

In the past, the most common approaches to solving these design problems were to hire an ex-Toyota guy as a consultant and hope he could figure it out, or go to a Toyota plant and hope you could copy what you see for your system, or throw up your hands and say "this will not work here." None of these options are very satisfying approaches. The ex-Toyota guy may not be able to translate the principles he saw at Toyota into your system. Copying what you see is doomed to failure, unless your conditions happen to be the same as those in the plant you visit. Those of us who get to see many different implementations of the Toyota Production System know how robust it is across many different industries, labor relations situations, and product demand conditions. In short, TPS will work in many places, but it has to be properly applied.

In the mid-1990s the companies trying to apply TPS were mostly auto and they were predominantly in the mode of copying and using ex-Toyota consultants. Little did they know that Toyota had developed a mapping method that could greatly improve their approach. The methodology was used extensively by Toyota's Operation Management Consulting Division in Japan, primarily to work with suppliers, and then used as a core tool by the Toyota Supplier Support Center in the U.S., which was set up to work with U.S. companies outside of Toyota plants. The map simply focused on the flow of material and information. At this point there were no organizational structures, nor technical details about individual processes. It was a 5,000 foot view of how material and information flows through your facility. You map the current situation and identify the waste that impedes the flow. There are a lot of ahas! You then develop a future-state vision with the help of icons peculiar to TPS. You then develop a detailed action plan to get to the future state—what, when, and who.

Toyota had TPS experts who did this analysis and often did not even share it with their clients. Mike Rother and John Shook took this methodology and made it available to the masses in their title *Learning to See*. This book has become a best seller in the lean publishing world because it helps put the pieces together, showing mere mortals how this method works in a system of material and information flow.

However, *Learning to See* does have its limitations. Its purpose was to introduce the icons, the drawing methodology, the philosophy, and the overall process of going from current, to future, to action plan. It did this and was a great primer on TPS to boot. It focused on a company that was very much like the cases the TPS experts in Toyota saw time after time. A typical supplier who ships direct to Toyota has the following characteristics:

1. A mature product changing in an evolutionary way: Minor changes every two to three years and significant redesign every four to six years is typical.
2. Mass production: Producing parts for a car a minute is not uncommon.
3. Limited part options: Tens of thousands of possible vehicle configurations, but made up of combinations of a few options for each component part (e.g., different color steering wheels).

4. Lots of small parts: Most can fit into totes.

5. Build for sale to the Toyota plant and few other customers.

6. A carefully leveled schedule: Toyota makes the same number and mix of cars every day over the month and works hard to keep the schedule level. This leads to a leveled demand for engines, body parts, and all supplied parts, and allows for minimum inventory in buffers.

7. A long-term contract with Toyota.

We are typically looking at a basic manufacturing operation. When you are trying to introduce a mapping methodology, a process, and a philosophy, why use a complex case example that has all kinds of exceptions to the rule and complex alternative solutions?

Nevertheless, unfortunately the world is not that simple. You may be selling to many customers, with varying requirements, who demand their product on short notice, who require highly engineered custom products, and who do not give you multi-year contracts. So what should you do? As a teacher and advisor in industry the most common question I get asked is: "What about me? My company is complex."

Fortunately, I can now answer this question by referencing *Creating Mixed Model Value Streams*. The book assumes you have some familiarity with value stream mapping, but that your situation is intricate and complicated. You have a high variety of products, some are customized, your demand may not be leveled, and strategically it may make sense for you to build to customer order. This book takes you through a clear step-by-step process using the case of Electro-Motion Control (EMC) Supply Company—"a manufacturer of a variety of parts and products for the motion control and electronic industries." Thank heaven we have moved out of automotive!

EMC makes a variety of products with a broad range of cycle times, faces varying demand, has some custom products, and needs to build to order as much as possible. Kevin Duggan is experienced in implementing lean in environments like this and walks us through the same reasoning he has used with great success in actual practice. This is not just a theoretical exercise. The reasoning is at a very detailed level, so it answers all of your frequently asked questions.

EMC decides that it can only afford to keep a small amount of a few high-volume products in a supermarket and has to build to order as much as possible. The author then walks us through the process of developing the future state, including balancing the flow for the mix, creating standard work for the mix, setting the pitch at the pacemaker, scheduling the mix at the pacemaker, and dealing with changes in customer demand. There is a lot of detail here and an attached CD includes a simple Excel template that will help you sort through your products to identify product families. You must isolate a product family with some limits on the range of variation in cycle times, or establishing flow will be hopeless.

Creating Mixed Model Value Streams is required reading for most firms that are serious about lean transformation. It not only addresses a critical need for companies in a high-variety product environment, but also covers many details in developing your lean system. It deals with more complex issues, but it is written clearly and presented in a very digestible form. It is one more step towards moving beyond copying what we see in Toyota plants and developing our own lean production systems.

Jeffrey K. Liker
University of Michigan

Preface

I remember the moment I began my lean journey. It was in the late 1980s. I was engineering manager for a company that produced injected molded parts on the first floor, decorated these parts on the third floor, then sent the parts seven miles across town to the assembly plant to pack them in a box. From there they were moved 30 miles to a warehouse. The parts continued to move through warehouses and distribution centers until they finally reached retail outlets.

I was standing next to a large molding press holding parts that were warped and damaged due to material handling and transportation. With me was Mr. Steve Jessup, who had recently taken over the operation of the factories. While I was suggesting ideas on how to better package the part at the press to avoid damage, Steve turned to me and said: "When you think about it, all we really want to do is mold, decorate, and pack these parts in a box. Why do we do all this other stuff?" My eyes were opened. *Thanks Steve!*

Two weeks later, the part came out of the press and moved on to the decorating machine—which we had moved from the third floor and set up right next to the molding press. From there the parts were packed immediately in the box and shipped. Not only was the damage issue solved, but many other problems (such as matching colors and part warping) were solved as well. It was not an easy change. I was constantly told: "The molding plant is the molding plant. Decorating and assembly belong someplace else!" However, my eyes were opened and I kept moving forward.

In 1996, the book *Lean Thinking* was written by Jim Womack and Dan Jones. They were able to communicate to executives and managers what I could not. Waste is everywhere, and we must change our way of thinking to eliminate it. Thanks, Jim and Dan, for helping me help others see waste and agree to attack it.

In 1998, the book *Learning to See* by Mike Rother and John Shook introduced a value stream visualization method called value stream mapping (VSM), and my vision greatly improved. At the time I had been working with different companies implementing flow and mixed model manufacturing. This book helped me develop new ways to teach lean, and I decided to contact the Lean Enterprise Institute regarding these techniques. I began working with them as an instructor while I continued to help companies implement lean. My teaching and learning skills quickly expanded, as I also became a Director for the Lean Enterprise Institute in Canada.

Over the years, I have learned that the secret to a successful lean implementation is not to apply lean tools to convert a company, but to teach a company how to see the sources of waste and guide them through a process to eliminate them. I often find that organizations understand the concepts but have difficulty applying them in their particular environments. Their shopfloors are more complicated than the teaching examples used. They have many different products, different cycle times, daily changing demand, and other variables that make it difficult to create a future state with less waste. For this reason, I decided (with the coaching of LEI Canada) to document a process for creating future states in a mixed model environment. I had been doing mixed model implementations, always teaching it from an "engineering perspective." The challenge was to describe the process so anyone could understand it.

In writing this book, I have assumed that readers have a basic knowledge of value stream mapping. If you have not, it may be a good idea to learn more about it from *Learning to See*[1] or the

---

1. *Learning to See*. Mike Rother and John Shook. The Lean Enterprise Institute, 1998.

educational series on VSM from Productivity, Inc. I will go into detail on creating future-state value streams. My focus will be from the crucial process of the pacemaker out to the customer, as this is the first place to begin implementing lean concepts into your value streams.

All this being said, my hope is that the pages to follow will help you learn more about lean and how to apply it in high-mix environments to eliminate waste. *Remember: To continue your lean journey, it is essential to keep asking questions!*

Kevin J. Duggan

Acknowledgments

This book would have not been possible without the help of my dedicated friend at the Lean Enterprise Institute in Canada, Mr. Steve Withers. Steve has spent many weekends, and evenings into the late hours, reading through manuscripts (and missing time with his family) to assist me in writing it. Constant discussions with Steve kept me focused on you, the reader. His feedback proved to be invaluable. Steve wouldn't always tell me if my work was good or bad, but he would always ask the right questions. By so doing, he kept me from writing some technical journal that engineers would love but others might find slow going.

Although the work that follows is mine, much of it was spawned from discussions with Steve. For this I give him my sincerest thanks for his hard work and efforts.

Besides Steve, there were others who were very helpful in this writing. I would like to thank my other friends at the Lean Enterprise Institute in Canada. Along with my associates Mr. Steve Pawlowicz and Mr. Brian Moffitt.

A final thanks to Mike Rother, who helped me to see the big picture through a sea of complexity and detail. Mike's ability to teach and write has helped me find new ways to communicate ideas to just about anyone, whether theat person has never heard of lean or has been on the lean journey for a lifetime.

PART I:
INTRODUCTION

❏ Getting Started
❏ Welcome to EMC Supply Company

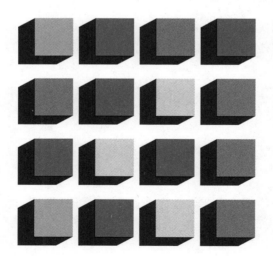

QUESTIONS FOR MIXED MODEL

1. Do we have the right product families?

2. What is the takt time at the pacemaker?

3. Can the equipment support the takt time?

4. What is the interval?

5. What are the operator balance charts for the products?

6. How will we balance flow for the mix?

7. How will we create standard work for the mix?

8. How will we create the pitch at the pacemaker?

9. How will we schedule the mix at the pacemaker?

10. How will we deal with changes in customer demand?

Getting Started

Lean is about eliminating waste. Waste is any activity that does not add value. Value is any activity that transforms the product in a way the customer is willing to pay for. Customers typically do not want to pay for overproduction, material handling, waiting, scrap, rework, inventory, overprocessing, or even inspection. These are all waste.

Before we can eliminate waste, we must be able to see it. If we can identify waste, we can target it for elimination. If we can't see it, it will remain.

In the book *Lean Thinking*,[1] five principles of lean are defined as follows:

1. Specify value.
2. Identify the value stream.
3. Make value flow.
4. Let customers pull.
5. Pursue perfection.

---

1. *Lean Thinking*. James P. Womack and Daniel T. Jones. Simon & Schuster, 1996, p.10. Note: *Lean Thinking* and *The Lean Enterprise* are trademarks of the Lean Enterprise Institute.

These principles help us identify waste and provide ways to help us to reduce it. First, we specify value from the customer, *as the customer always defines value*. Then we map the flow of value. Once we map the flow of value we develop and implement a future state where value will flow, without stopping and accumulating, to the customer. Customers may then pull (or signal us their needs), and we would flow value only when this happens. To complete the cycle, we repeatedly create new future-state maps and continuously improve as we pursue perfection.

Over recent years, many companies have learned to visualize and redesign their flow of value using value stream mapping.[2] Value stream mapping enables all employees to see sources of waste and develop future states that greatly reduce it.

By now, value stream mapping is a common term in the manufacturing vocabulary. As a quick review, a value stream comprises all the actions (both value-added and non-value-added) currently required to bring a product through the main flows essential to every product: (1) the design flow from the concept of a new product to the launch, and (2) the production flow from raw material into the hands of the customer.[3]

The act of creating value stream maps (both current state and future state) is itself waste, or non-value-added. The only value provided is when we *implement* a future state with less waste—in other words, when we begin to *make value flow*.

Flow manufacturing (building the product in a continuous manner without any stoppages or backtracking) is the best way to manufacture with the least amount of waste. We should always try to create continuous one-piece flow first, and where we can't flow (e.g., a supplier of raw material), we should implement pull through a signaling method such as kanban.

Flow manufacturing is not a new concept. If we retrace the history of lean thinking, we find that Henry Ford was one of the pioneers of flow. Ford's 1913 factory in Highland Park had but one product—the Model T—and no product variation at all. In some years you could have any color you wanted, *as long as it was black*! Creating

---

2. Value stream mapping is taught in the book *Learning to See* by Mike Rother and John Shook. The Lean Enterprise Institute, 1998.

3. *Learning to See*. Mike Rother and John Shook. The Lean Enterprise Institute, 1998, p.3.

flow in such an environment is much simpler than in a factory with many products and many options. Indeed, Ford's flow concepts died in the late 1920s essentially because customers wanted numerous options. As a result, traditional mass production in departments was implemented in Ford's River Rouge plant. Later, in the 1940s and 1950s, Toyota actually developed a production system for making products in lower volumes with high variety. Although these concepts were pioneered and proven in the automotive industry, they have been and continue to be applied in a wide array of industries.

So flow is not new. However, many companies have struggled with implementing flow. Their implementation seems to stall. When they look at the complexity of their environment, they do not know where to begin, and too many questions are left unanswered. Product variety and mix, along with constant demand changes, make the basic concepts of flow used by Henry Ford in 1913 difficult to implement. It is often said that Toyota can achieve flow in a mixed environment because, as an automotive company, it can level the demand for months to create a stable mix for their factories. Companies that are high mix in a nonautomotive supply chain say that they simply cannot apply the lean tools of flow and pull in their dynamic environments.

This book explains how to create flow in these environments and how to begin flow with the pull of the customer. We will focus on the creation of future-state value stream designs in a high-mix environment. In the development of our future-state designs, we will step away from the automotive industry to apply these concepts to a demanding, high-pace supplier who must fulfill changing demand each day.

CHALLENGES OF THE REAL FACTORY

Very few factories can afford to purchase and dedicate machinery to each product. Equipment is commonly used to build multiple products. In a sense, almost all factories run a mix of products through the same equipment, over some amount of time. When the number of products increases while the time to run these products decreases, complexity sets in. We often try to offset these complexities with better scheduling systems which in turn adds to the complexity.

Some of the difficulty in implementing flow and pull in real-life factories may be found in the following areas.

High Product Mix

Flow can be hard to see when products have a multitude of options, variations in both lead times and cycle times, and intertwining between multiple processes. A high variety of products or services may make it difficult to determine product families. It is hard to tell which equipment can be dedicated to a product family and which equipment must be shared across multiple product families. A high mix of products that share the same line or equipment also makes it much harder to schedule due to availability of machinery and capacity. Complex MRP schedules often lead to higher inventories on the floor, which in turn lead to longer lead times, missing parts, increased costs, frustration, lack of control, and constant fire-fighting. Visibility on the workfloor becomes impossible, and managers can't tell how the factory is performing. Identifying and managing bottlenecks becomes a full-time job.

Shared Resources

Almost all factories have shared equipment (i.e., stamping machines, ovens, injection molding presses). These can be very capital intensive and are usually monitored tightly from an accounting standpoint. Measurements such as machine utilization, variance, and productivity are the reasons for large batch sizes to "optimize the machine." Scheduling then attempts to avoid setups by combining runs. Lot sizes are determined by "economic order quantities." Parts are produced whether the next process needs them or not. Changeovers are carried out, depending upon which salesman screams the loudest. All of this is done in order to optimize internal resources. By the way, where is the focus in this system? I believe you will find the focus in this system is on process maximization instead of on flow optimization.

Information Flows

In a manufacturing environment, information flow (scheduling) may be very difficult to see and may seem to change by the minute. Operators and supervisors constantly review inventories and priorities and adjust the schedule dynamically. Production control seeks accurate, by-the-minute counts to key into MRP systems in order to plan around equipment failures and part shortages.

A New Look at These Challenges with Value Stream Mapping

In order to create flow, we must first see it. One of the best tools to see flow is value stream mapping. Value stream mapping is a visualization method that allows us to map the flow of value from raw material to the customer. It was introduced by Mike Rother and John Shook in their book, *Learning to See*.[4] The premise of value stream mapping is to understand flow from the customer's perspective. Imagine that we place a red sticker on a piece of raw material (such as a coil of steel, or bar stock) when it arrives at the factory. We can track this piece through all of the activities (those that add value and those that do not add value) until it is shipped to the customer. We would observe processing steps and inventory accumulation.

Value stream mapping is performed in the following manner:[5]

☐ Select a product family.
☐ Create a current-state map.
☐ Create a future-state map using lean techniques.
☐ Create an implementation plan for the future state.
☐ Implement the future state through structured continuous improvement activities.

Value stream maps are created on the shopfloor. By taking a tour of the shopfloor, we can identify process steps (process starting and ending points are identified where flow stops and inventory accumulates). We then record the data for each process in a data box beneath each process. The typical data needed is:

☐ Cycle time (how often does a piece come out of the process)
☐ Changeover time (time from the last good piece of product A until the next good piece of product B)
☐ Uptime (how often the machine is in good working order when we need it)
☐ Number of operators

---

4. *Learning to See*. Mike Rother and John Shook. The Lean Enterprise Institute, 1998.

5. *Learning to See*. Mike Rother and John Shook. The Lean Enterprise Institute, 1998, p. 7.

We also record any inventory at the process step (no matter where it is located) and illustrate this by using an inventory-warning triangle. The inventory quantity is recorded below the triangle. We also document how material flows from one process to the next. If material is sent to the next process, whether it is needed it or not, then a push arrow is used.

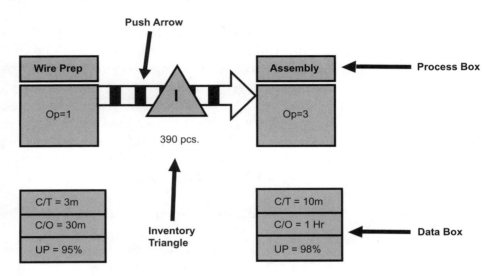

After material flows are captured, we record information flow. A good way to capture information flow is to ask the question, "How does the operator know what to build next?" If the operator must review the schedule, then an information arrow (solid line for paper, jagged for electronic) should be drawn to represent the schedule from production control to the process. We also show the information flow between customers and suppliers (three-month forecast, daily faxes, etc.). For the full mapping icons chart, please see the inside front cover.

After material and information flows have been recorded, we measure flow through the value stream by creating a lead-time ladder at the bottom of the value stream map. This ladder compares the amount of lead time (due to inventory) to the process time to create the part. As we create the lead-time ladder, we value the inventory recorded in terms of days (or other lengths of time), not pieces. We convert the inventory pieces to time by asking, "How long will this inventory be here if it is consumed at the rate at which the customer buys it?" At the end of the ladder, we summarize the total amount of lead time compared to the total amount of process time. This sends a powerful message, that can be read as: "The customer wants to buy 18 minutes worth of work from us, and it takes us 32.6 days to deliver it!"

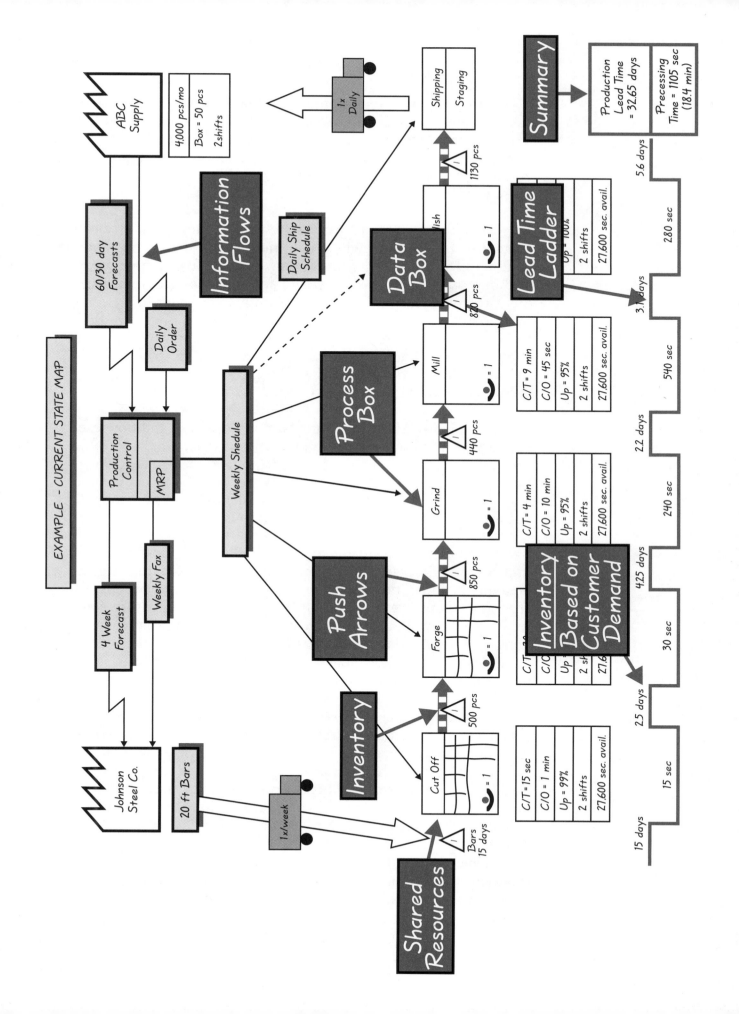

Once a good current state is established, the next step is to create a lean future state with less waste. This is done by following some lean guidelines such as takt (the customer demand rate), continuous flow, pull, scheduling only one point, leveling mix and volume, and providing a management timeframe. We will cover these guidelines (and more) in great detail throughout this text.

We will draw a new future-state map to illustrate these concepts, identifying areas where continuous flow will be present and where pull will be needed. As we develop the future state we will find that targeted improvements in specific areas are needed in order to apply lean concepts. For example, we might like a machine to directly feed an assembly station in a one-piece flow fashion, but the current changeover time of the machine will not allow for this. Therefore, we would place a kaizen (continuous improvement) burst around the machine stating that changeover time must be reduced to one minute.

We will also show new information flows that tell how each operator will know what to build next, and what single point in the value stream will be the schedule point or pacemaker. The future state does not have to have all the answers. It is dynamic and will change as we progress. Eventually, the future state will become the current state as we continuously improve.

Finally, after our future state is complete, we develop an implementation plan. This is done by taking the future state and breaking it down into implementation loops. We draw loops around areas where flow and pull are needed in our future state; we list the kaizen events needed in each loop in a project plan, tying each improvement to a business objective; and we establish a physically measurable goal (e.g., zero inventory between processes) that lets us know easily when the goal is attained.

By following the process of value stream mapping (select a product family, create a current-state map, create a future-state map, and then form an implementation plan), we avoid doing random kaizen events that do not bring any results to the bottom line. The value stream map provides structured continuous improvement that will lead us into a lean value stream and provide us with a continuous improvement culture.

Value stream mapping is an excellent way to get everyone to see their value streams and agree to eliminate waste. Applying lean guidelines such as takt, flow, pull, and leveling will streamline the value stream and reduce inventory. The difficulty lies in applying these guidelines in factories that have a high mix of products that must travel through the same value stream. In these cases we will need more detail and will have to develop some new tools to apply lean guidelines in this environment. For more information on value stream mapping, refer to *Learning to See* by Mike Rother and John Shook in the "Important Sources" section on p. 189.

WHERE DO WE START?

When we discuss mixed model value streams, we are discussing companies that have hundreds of products they must produce through the same value stream. To teach the concepts of lean in this environment, we will use a product family containing only nine products. The same concepts apply if the product family contains hundreds of products. We will cover the "door-to-door" production flow of a complex and high-variety value stream at the EMC Supply Company. We will work at the plant level and stay within the four walls of EMC Supply, where our focus will be to create a mixed model pacemaker that can react to meet changing customer demand. (The pacemaker is the one process where we will schedule the value stream, p. 47.)

We will first select a product family, then overview the current-state map for this family. We will spend most of our time creating a future-state map, as this is where the challenge lies. As we will soon discover, some product families at the EMC Supply Company are not simple. Our first step will be to define a product family within EMC Supply, and then map the value stream for this product family. Although the value stream may be complex, we can use a pencil and paper to draw a visual representation of both the flow of material and information as the product makes its way through the value stream. We will then ask a set of key questions and develop a future state that is capable of producing a high variety of products, at the pull of the customer, with minimal waste. Let's get started.

Welcome to EMC Supply Company

The Electro-Motion Control (EMC) Supply Company is a manufacturer that produces a high variety of parts and products for the motion control and electronic industries. Their motion control products support various control valves and linkages used in the food and petroleum industries. Their products include motion controllers, P.C. boards, electrical/mechanical assemblies, actuators, diverters, control arms, linkages, motors, servos, sensors, interfacing software, and other related products. In addition to a standard product line of motion controllers, they produce spare parts and custom parts per customer specifications. The customer's equipment (which is often a very expensive system) is usually down and awaiting a replacement part from EMC Supply. Therefore, the customer expects parts to ship the day they are ordered.

EMC Supply has a sister company (J&J Forming) that produces distributor caps for the automotive industry. J&J Forming has recently applied lean principles to its production of distributor caps and has shown considerable success in reducing lead times and increasing on-time delivery. After the visible success at J&J Forming, corporate management has directed EMC Supply to implement lean principles. The plant management at EMC Supply agrees with the direction and would also like similar results to those attained at J&J Forming, but they are unsure how to proceed in their complex environment. EMC management believes that lean has worked well for J&J Forming due to the limited number of products, steadier demand, dedicated equipment, and a leveled schedule for the automotive world.

There are a number of processes at EMC Supply, including stamping, injection molding, welding, electrical assembly, mechanical assembly, deburring, painting, and testing. At present, these processes are organized by department as the equipment is used to make a variety of products. EMC Supply is functionally organized with department managers and is heavily controlled by MRP (Material Requirements Planning) and MRP II (Manufacturing Resource Planning). EMC has late deliveries and frequently works overtime to keep up. When you observe the workplace everyone seems to be busy. Machine utilization, productivity, and efficiency are monitored in each department. Supervisors are always working to keep machines and people busy (which is very important to EMC Supply). As a result, machine utilization is high and productivity seems good. However, due to shrinking margins, the management is under increasing pressures to reduce cost *and* shorten lead times.

Corporate management has created a timeline for EMC to improve their business performance. In their efforts to attain the timeline handed down from corporate management, EMC managers created current-state and future-state maps. To the untrained eye, these maps showed good progress at EMC Supply. The maps were very busy in the current state, and much cleaner in the future state. However, none of the managers understood the future state (or how to implement it), but they wanted to start seeing the gains made at J&J Forming in their own factory very soon.

EMC managers need to begin implementation of their future state (to meet the deadlines), but the high variety of products and constantly changing demand has caused them to hesitate. They have designed cells, but forming these cells will use equipment needed for other products. This has led to endless discussions with the department managers on the need for more capital investment in equipment before starting. Additionally, the confusion has led to questions like, "Who is responsible for what area? Which products are more important? Which customers can wait?"

Knowing their next visit from corporate management is but a few weeks away, EMC managers have invited us to visit their factory and assist them with their lean implementation.

OUR VISIT TO EMC SUPPLY

When we arrived at EMC Supply, we were greeted by members of the management team and immediately brought to a conference room. Everyone began talking (seemingly all at once), explaining the complexities and uniqueness of their operation. Although some saw potential improvements, the basic consensus was that the lean principles used at J&J Forming could not be applied to their complex operation. They explained to us that automotive products were only a small part of their business while their demand was for a high variety of products, including custom orders, which change daily. They stated they have no idea what the customer will order the next day, so they try to keep stock available to ship the same day. They use a three-month forecast that is a good guess at best. They felt their high-mix environment with variations in demand, demanding customers, custom orders, and shared processing equipment could not be viewed in the same way as J&J Forming. Nor could EMC Supply hope to realize the same level of improvement as their sister company through the application of lean principles. They wanted our help explaining this to corporate management. Although the managers would have continued to discuss this all morning, we suggested a visit to the shopfloor so we could see for ourselves.

In order to understand process flow, we asked a few key questions during our tour:

- ❏ How does this operator know what to build next?
- ❏ What will the operator do when the machine stops?
- ❏ Where will the finished pieces be sent to next?
- ❏ Where do operators get the raw material?
- ❏ How many products will they cycle through per day?
- ❏ How long will it be before they make this part again?
- ❏ Why is this material waiting?
- ❏ How are operators doing compared to where they should be on the schedule?

After our review of the floor it was easy to see the difficulty the managers were facing. Piles of mixed inventory were found throughout the floor. Parts were tagged as "Due Today," "Hot," "Red Hot," etc. No flow seemed to exist as the equipment was shared and produced a large variety of parts in batches. Although the managers had told us a constant backlog of 7 to 10 days existed, we found completed orders on the shipping dock that were not due until next month. Negotiating between production control, operators, supervisors, and department heads occurred as to which job should be done next. We observed that some work areas had no employees. When we asked why, we found that they were seeking the necessary tools to do a setup. Each department head was concerned with optimizing his or her area for the amount of variety needed. Territorial management seemed to be the norm, with the better negotiator (usually the one with the bigger hammer) succeeding.

After seeing the shopfloor and reviewing some data with the team, we headed back to the conference room. Once there, the managers displayed their attempts to organize the spaghetti into value streams and map them. They voiced their frustration at using these techniques in their environment. They did not understand how lean techniques could help them manage the day-to-day chaos in their factory.

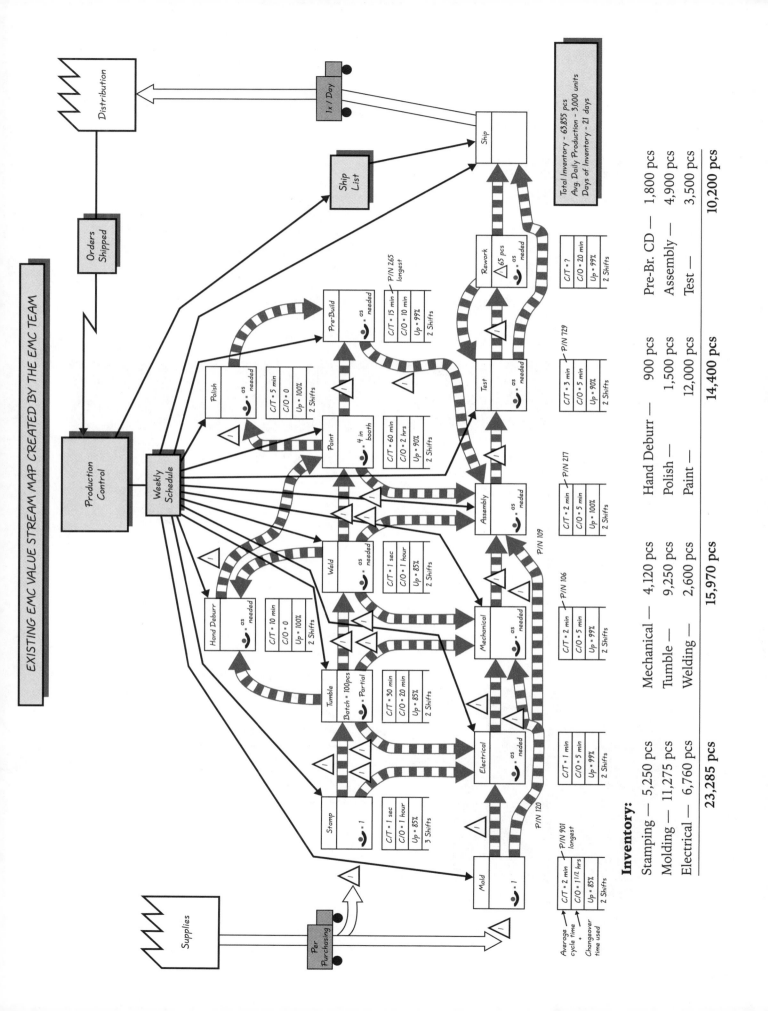

EXISTING EMC VALUE STREAM MAP CREATED BY THE EMC TEAM

Inventory:

Stamping — 5,250 pcs   Mechanical — 4,120 pcs   Hand Deburr — 900 pcs   Pre-Br. CD — 1,800 pcs

Molding — 11,275 pcs   Tumble — 9,250 pcs   Polish — 1,500 pcs   Assembly — 4,900 pcs

Electrical — 6,760 pcs   Welding — 2,600 pcs   Paint — 12,000 pcs   Test — 3,500 pcs

23,285 pcs   15,970 pcs   14,400 pcs   10,200 pcs

Total Inventory – 63,855 pcs
Avg. Daily Production – 3,000 units
Days of Inventory – 21 days

We began by explaining our thoughts on this situation using our chaos graph.

The Chaos Graph

The chaos graph simply shows the relationship of lead time to chaos. Plotted on a curve, the relationship between lead time and chaos becomes apparent. The longer the lead time, the more chaos enters into the system. Long lead times make it almost impossible to predict what is needed far enough in advance. To verify this, simply ask the question, "What do we need to build three months from now?" Follow that with, "What do we need to build tomorrow?" Which answer do we think will be more accurate? We will find that the answer to the second question is indeed more accurate.

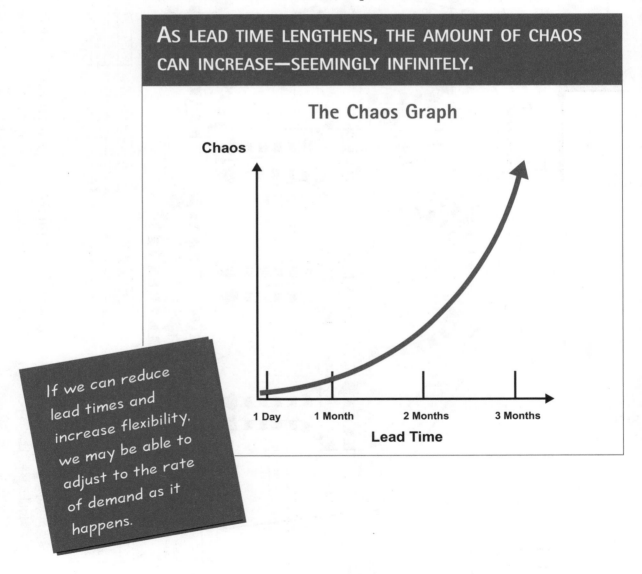

AS LEAD TIME LENGTHENS, THE AMOUNT OF CHAOS CAN INCREASE—SEEMINGLY INFINITELY.

The Chaos Graph

Chaos

1 Day   1 Month   2 Months   3 Months

Lead Time

If we can reduce lead times and increase flexibility, we may be able to adjust to the rate of demand as it happens.

The bottom line in all this can be summed up as follows: *The shorter the lead time, the more accurate the forecast.*

This simple explanation helped them understand how eliminating waste and reducing lead time will impact the forecasting and scheduling of their operation. However, they were doubtful that lean principles could do this in their environment as it did at J&J Forming.

Our next task was to explain that the lean principles applied at their sister company could apply at their facility. However, their situation was more complex and a further understanding of their business was needed. We began with a few questions:

What Kind of Manufacturer Is EMC?

The first thing we need to do before we can begin to apply lean principles is to understand what type of manufacturer EMC Supply Company is. Do they manufacture discrete parts with steady demand? Do they manufacture discrete parts with a high variety and variable demand? Do they customize products per order? We will focus the conversation by value stream, not on the entire operation. We start with an illustration to help the EMC team decide the mode for their products.

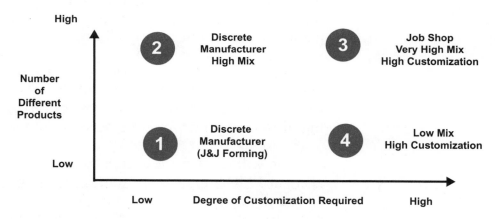

The EMC team identified themselves as being closest to number two—a discrete manufacturer of high-mix products with some customization of products. We then asked them for a demand profile for the majority of their products. By demand profile, we mean the degree of unpredictability of demand over a period of time. We provided a few illustrations of this, as follows. (See the figure on the next page.)

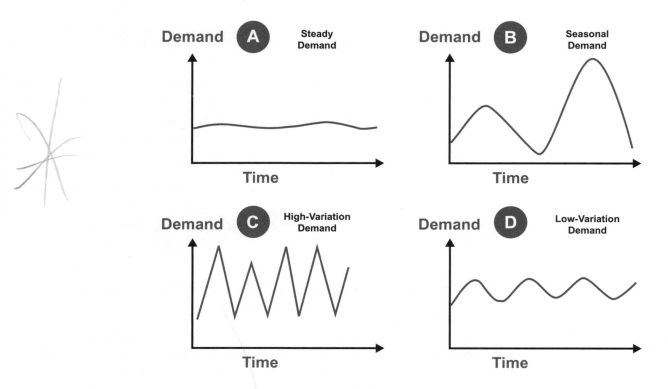

EMC looked back at actual shipments over the past 12 months and identified themselves with type C, high-variation demand over a short amount of time. We next asked them the status of their finished-goods inventory. They responded they had plenty of goods, but mostly all the wrong items.

After we determined together that EMC's business would be one of high-mix and high-demand changes over a short period of time, we realized that the concepts of mixed model manufacturing, flow, and pull, would be needed in this environment.

We will explain these concepts to you as we did to the managers at EMC Supply by posing 10 questions you should address as you develop your future state. We will "sweat the details," in order to deeply understand the complexity and simplify it into lean guidelines of flow, pull, and leveling. These details will require careful attention by the entire team, but the result will lead to a greater understanding of applying lean principles in a complex environment. We will start with an overview of mixed model production.

MIXED MODEL PRODUCTION

Mixed model production means producing a variety or mix of products or product variations through the same value stream *at the pull of the customer*. This means to build and deliver the right quantity of a specific product (out of a high number of products available) when the customer wants it.

A mix of products flows through the same value stream.

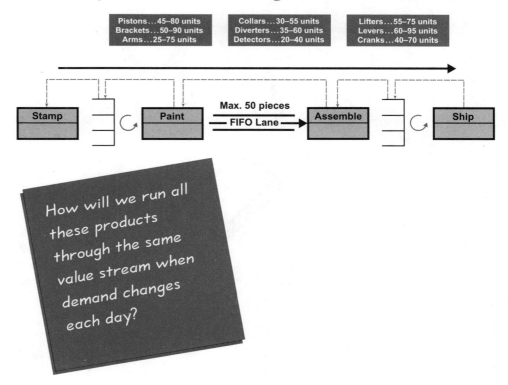

In mixed model production, a group of products are determined to be a product family and are treated as one. This means that we review the total volume for a product family rather than the individual demand for each product in the family to see if we can ship the orders needed each day.

As an example, consider a product family of clamps. Each product (A, B, and C) goes through the processes of casting, threading, and assembly. The total demand for all three clamps is 1,000 units per day.

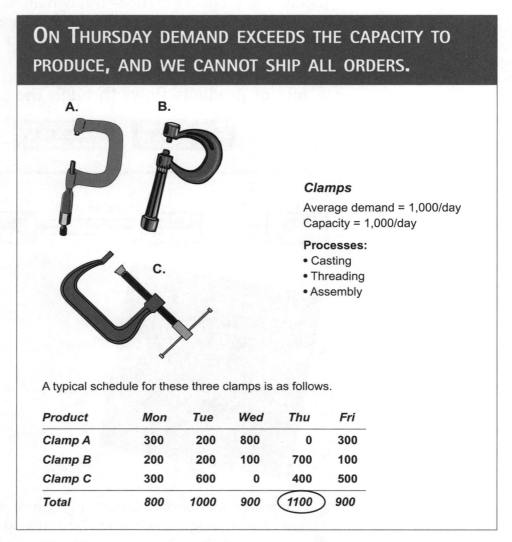

ON THURSDAY DEMAND EXCEEDS THE CAPACITY TO PRODUCE, AND WE CANNOT SHIP ALL ORDERS.

A. B. C.

Clamps

Average demand = 1,000/day
Capacity = 1,000/day

Processes:
• Casting
• Threading
• Assembly

A typical schedule for these three clamps is as follows.

Product	Mon	Tue	Wed	Thu	Fri
Clamp A	300	200	800	0	300
Clamp B	200	200	100	700	100
Clamp C	300	600	0	400	500
Total	800	1000	900	1100	900

Let's look at a second product family of wrenches. Each wrench (A, B, and C) goes through the processes of casting, threading, and assembly. The total volume for all three wrenches is 2,000 units per day.

ON MONDAY DEMAND EXCEEDS THE CAPACITY TO PRODUCE, AND WE CANNOT SHIP ALL ORDERS.

Wrenches

Average demand = 2,000/day
Capacity = 2,000/day

Processes:
- Casting
- Threading
- Assembly

A typical schedule for these three wrenches is as follows.

Product	Mon	Tue	Wed	Thu	Fri
Wrench 1	900	200	1000	800	600
Wrench 2	600	600	500	400	1000
Wrench 3	600	900	500	700	400
Total	2100	1700	2000	1900	2000

Could we combine these six products into one product family and create one value stream? Would there be advantages to this?

WRENCHES AND CLAMPS PRODUCT FAMILY (MIXED MODEL LINE)

Product	Mon	Tue	Wed	Thu	Fri
Clamp A	300	200	800	0	300
Clamp B	200	200	100	700	100
Clamp C	300	600	0	400	500
Wrench 1	900	200	1000	800	600
Wrench 2	600	600	500	400	1000
Wrench 3	600	900	500	700	400
Total	2900	2700	2900	3000	2900

All orders were shipped this week.

Clamps and Wrenches Product Family

Average demand = 3,000/day
Capacity = 3,000/day

Processes:
- Casting
- Threading
- Assembly

Combining products with the same processing steps into a product family makes us more flexible in responding to customer demand. As demand increases for one product, it may decrease for another, allowing more capability to respond to changing customer demands.

By creating one product family of wrenches and clamps with a total volume of 3,000 units per day, all orders are now shipped on time. We added flexibility to build the right products at the right time by increasing the number of products in the mix and increasing the total volume. When demand is down for one product, we can build another product whose demand has increased. This eliminates the waste of overproduction and inventory while increasing on-time delivery.

In certain cases, some mixes may become unmanageable due to the mix of products and their respective work content. This may require overtime, extra staffing, or a *leveled mix* (we will discuss this later in the book, pp. 144–146).

EMC's Thoughts on Mixed Model Production

The management team at EMC Supply Co. understood our simple example using clamps and wrenches. However, they were not too sure how we could apply this to their products. To put things in perspective for them, we created a quick example on the whiteboard using their products. We did not know at this point what their product families were. To create an example, we asked them to give us names of some of their products that used electrical components. They named products that used sensors and detectors.

We further explained that *if* we could create a product family of sensors and detectors, and understand the total demand for this product family, we could then create a chart, as follows.

The total demand for this product family for one day is 275 units. We understand that the demand for individual products might increase or decrease each day. In fact, we are counting on it. If we use the highest volume of each part, this may require us to buy extra machines and equipment that would not be consistently needed. It would be better to treat the family as a group, knowing that when demand goes up for one part, it will tend to decrease for another.

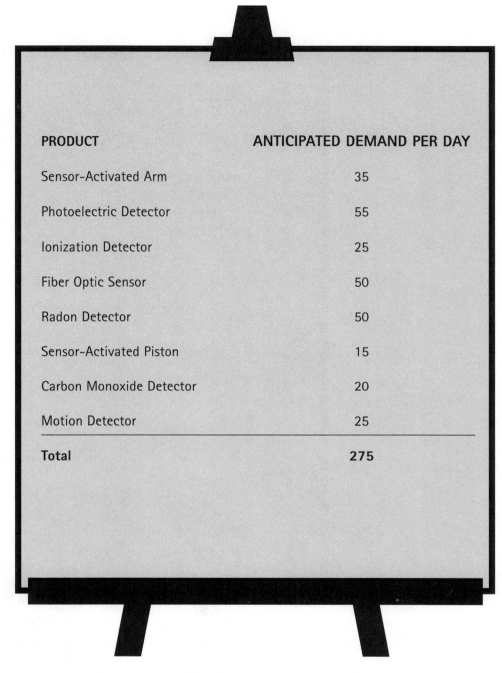

PRODUCT	ANTICIPATED DEMAND PER DAY
Sensor-Activated Arm	35
Photoelectric Detector	55
Ionization Detector	25
Fiber Optic Sensor	50
Radon Detector	50
Sensor-Activated Piston	15
Carbon Monoxide Detector	20
Motion Detector	25
Total	**275**

In our future-state development, we would strive to create a value stream that could produce a maximum of 275 units of any mix. In general, if the demand exceeded 275 units, we would have to work overtime, add staffing, or level the mix. Once the future state value stream was implemented, the product family could respond to daily orders as shown on the next page.

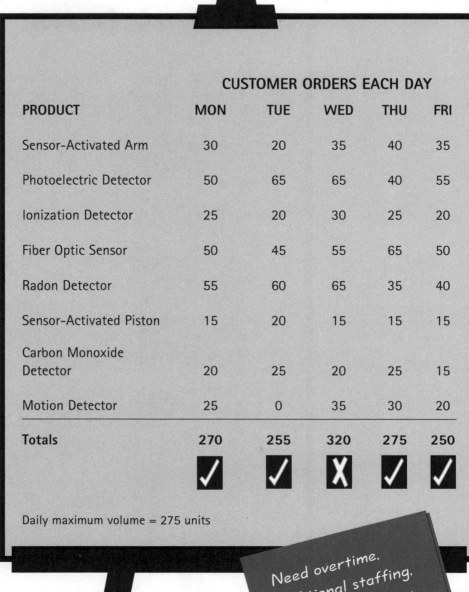

PRODUCT	CUSTOMER ORDERS EACH DAY				
	MON	TUE	WED	THU	FRI
Sensor-Activated Arm	30	20	35	40	35
Photoelectric Detector	50	65	65	40	55
Ionization Detector	25	20	30	25	20
Fiber Optic Sensor	50	45	55	65	50
Radon Detector	55	60	65	35	40
Sensor-Activated Piston	15	20	15	15	15
Carbon Monoxide Detector	20	25	20	25	15
Motion Detector	25	0	35	30	20
Totals	**270**	**255**	**320**	**275**	**250**
	✓	✓	✗	✓	✓

Daily maximum volume = 275 units

Need overtime, additional staffing, or a leveled mix on Wednesday.

This illustration showed the EMC management team how the mixed model process could respond to their changing customer demand. The team was intrigued with these concepts and anxious to learn more and get started right away. They were surprised when we told them the first steps are to select a product family and create a good current-state value stream map. They had created a current-state map already (see page 17), so we began a detailed review of it.

Upon our review of their map, it quickly became obvious that their difficulty started right at step one, selecting the product family. They had mapped various parts through the factory; each of them intertwined between different processes. When we asked what product family a part belonged to, a variety of different answers were provided. Many felt that each product was different and could not be placed in a specific family.

We had to back up a little and discuss the development of product families in their high-mix environment. This needed to be done prior to drawing a correct current-state map for EMC Supply. It was time for us to start asking the 10 key questions for their future-state development.

SUMMARY

In mixed model production, any mix of products for a product family can be produced, as long as the total volume does not exceed total family volume. This means that only total demand needs to be reviewed to see if the orders can be filled. If the total is exceeded, the mix may still be made by working overtime, adding staffing, adding a shift (long term), leveling the mix, leveling the volume, buying more equipment (long term), and/or carrying inventory.

Mixed model is really a countermeasure to variability. We apply mixed model techniques where variability is high, as mixed model is very flexible and can respond to the variability as needed. Therefore, it is not necessary for a consistent, level schedule for lean principles to apply.

The key to planning mixed model manufacturing is selecting the right product family, understanding the total demand for the product family, and treating it as one product for scheduling.

What Have We Done So Far with the EMC Team?

So far, we have explained to the management team:

- ❏ What type of manufacturer they are
- ❏ What mixed model production entails
- ❏ Where it can be applied to their operation

We have let them see how mixed model concepts could fit their business and provide the flexibility they need.

What's Next for the Team?

Next we need to teach the management team how to determine product families in their high-variety environment. In a high-mix environment, specifying the product family may take some time and thought, and maybe a few new tools. Once we determine product families, we can select one to create a current-state map.

PART II:
PRODUCT FAMILIES AND THE PACEMAKER

- ❐ Question 1—Do We Have the Right Product Families?
- ❐ Question 2—What Is the Takt Time at the Pacemaker?
- ❐ Question 3—Can the Equipment Support the Takt Time?
- ❐ Question 4—What Is the Interval?

QUESTION 1–
Do We Have the Right Product Families?

PRODUCT FAMILIES—A CLOSER LOOK

A product family is a group of products that pass through similar processes or equipment and have similar work content. Shared resources are machines that produce components for more than one product family. It's best to consider a product family as a group of products that passes through similar *downstream* processing. By *downstream processing,* we mean the flow of product to the customer after the shared resources. To identify where downstream begins, start with the customer and move towards raw materials. Look for the point where continuous flow must end and pull, due to shared resources or unreliable equipment, must begin.

A product family matrix can help us identify product families. It can be a simple visual tool or a complex mathematical tool depending upon the application. The product family matrix is a grid that contains a list of processes in the columns and a list of products in the rows.

Processing Steps (Shared Resources) Upstream			Processing Steps (Dedicated Equipment) Downstream						
Products	**1**	**2**	**3**	**4**	**5**	**6**	**7**	**8**	**9**	**10**
A	X		X	X	X	X		X	X	
B	X	X		X	X	X	X	X	X	
C		X	X	X	X	X		X	X	X
D	X	X	X		X	X	X			X
E	X		X		X	X	X			X
F	X	X		X		X		X	X	X
CUSTOM	**X**	**X**	**X**	**X**		**X**		**X**	**X**	**X**

For custom products we may have to look upstream, as these processing steps may influence the downstream processing steps...

Following process flow may also be difficult. In certain cases, products may flow out of one process to the next, and then back to the first process. For example, a part might flow through these processes: stamp, deburr, grind, drill, deburr. In this case, list the deburr column as many times as this action takes place in order to show the product flow.

Product Flow →

Products	Stamp	Deburr	Grind	Drill	Deburr
A	X	X	X	X	X
B	X	X		X	X
C	X	X	X		X

The processing steps are placed in the columns. For example, stamping may be considered a process and may have its own column. But there may be many stamping presses, such as 500-ton, 750-ton, and 1,000-ton. Since a part that is produced in a 750-ton press cannot be produced in a 500-ton press, these press categories need separate columns. Remember to ask: "Could the 500-ton press make these parts, or did we just decide years ago to do it this way out of convenience?" Indicate *alternate machines* (machines that could also run the product but are not the primary choice due to slower speeds, setup, etc.) with an "A" (alternate) for future-state development if a part can be produced in one or more machines. Only one column is needed if all the machinery within a process is universal and any part can be made in any machine within the process. If there are multiple alternate processes, you may have to label each alternate A1, A2, A3, and so on.

Products	500T Stamp	Tumble Deburr	Flatbed Grind	Hand Grind	Hand Deburr	Drill Press	Tumble Deburr
A	X	X	X	(A)	X	X	X
B	X	X				X	X
C	X	X	X	(A)	X		

Enter an "A" for an alternate process.

When selecting products to place in the grid, it may be easier to place only the base model number for the models produced in the rows (e.g., 902—XX, where XX means slight derivations of the model that do not impact the manufacturing processing steps). Different models of the same product may represent only packaging changes, different graphics, different languages for instructions, and other non-process-related items. If a different model represents a change in processing steps, then each model should be listed under the product column.

DEVELOPING THE PRODUCT FAMILY MATRIX AT EMC

After working with the team at EMC Supply, we were able to put together a list of products and processing steps in order to develop their product family matrix. We found out that several products that normally go through the machine deburr department can alternately go through a hand deburr process.

Now the product family matrix can be sorted visually, so products with similar downstream processes are grouped together. Remember, by downstream (starting with the customer and moving towards raw materials) we mean the point where

Product Family Matrix at EMC Supply Company

Flow Ends/Pull Begins

Shared Equipment ←   → **Downstream (Flow)**

Product Family Matrix

P/N	Product Name	Injection Mold	Stamp	Deburr	Hand Deburr	Paint	Weld	Mechanical Assy.	Electrical Assy.	Final Assy.	Configure & Test	Ship
12834	XS2 Servo Motor	X	X			X			X		X	X
18392	Sensor-Activated Arm	X	X	X	A	X	X	X	X	X	X	X
19283	Photoelectric Detector					X			X		X	X
19299	Ionization Detector					X	X		X		X	X
21000	Laser-Activated Arm	X	X	X	A	X	X	X	X	X	X	X
21032	Manual Servo Motor	X	X			X			X		X	X
21042	Manual Servo Motor II	X	X			X			X		X	X
22020	Manually Activated Arm	X	X	X	A	X	X	X	X	X	X	X
23756	Fiber Optic Visual Sensor					X	X	X	X		X	X
24783	XS3 Servo Motor	X	X			X			X		X	X
25030	Radon Detector					X			X		X	X
28121	Barcode Diverter Piston	X	X	X	A	X	X	X	X	X	X	X
30000	Barcode Diverter Arm	X	X	X	A	X	X	X	X	X	X	X
31000	Sensor-Activated Piston	X	X	X	A	X	X	X	X	X	X	X
31666	Laser Diverter	X	X	X	A	X	X	X	X	X	X	X
32220	XS4 Servo Motor	X	X			X			X		X	X
34556	Carbon Monoxide Detector	X	X	X		X			X		X	X
35599	Auto Servo Motor	X	X	X		X			X		X	X
38200	Laser-Activated Piston	X	X	X	A	X	X	X	X	X	X	X
42005	Manually Activated Piston	X	X	X	A	X	X	X	X	X	X	X
45890	Motion Detector					X			X		X	X

Shared Equipment ←   → **Downstream (Flow)**

Flow Ends/Pull Begins

continuous flow must end and pull begins. Even though the paint booth is shared, parts are placed on hooks and can flow through in a continuous fashion.

Products in a product family do not have to follow the exact same process path. Process steps may be skipped or added, as some products may have options. At this point we are looking for products that require about 80 percent of the same downstream processing steps to be grouped into product families.

The next illustration shows the EMC product family matrix grouped into three product families. Each grouping does not necessarily go through identical processes. EMC decided to start by focusing on the first of the three groups in the table.

After grouping the products together, we can label them for easier identification. In this case we have created three product families, A, B, and C. We should also note that knowledge of the products is needed when grouping them together. For example, product 19283 Photoelectric Detector in family C goes through the same processing steps as family B. However, the team at EMC Supply know that this product cannot run on the same line due to dust contamination, so it must run with the products in family C.

If a product family matrix contains hundreds of products it may be very difficult to sort them visually. In this case it may be easier to create the matrix in a computer and use some logic to sort them. One method for sorting a large number of products into product families with mathematical weighting is covered in a tutorial included on the accompanying CD.

EMC Supply Company
Sorted Product Family Matrix

Focused Product Family

	Product Name	Hand Deburr	Paint	Weld	Mechanical Assy.	Electrical Assy.	Final Assy.	Configure & Test	Ship	Family
18392	Sensor-Activated Arm	X	X	X	X	X	X	X	X	A
21000	Laser-Activated Arm	X	X	X	X	X	X	X	X	A
22020	Manually Activated Arm	X	X	X	X	X	X	X	X	A
28121	Barcode Diverter Piston	X	X	X	X	X	X	X	X	A
30000	Barcode Diverter Arm	X	X	X	X	X	X	X	X	A
31000	Sensor-Activated Piston	X	X	X	X	X	X	X	X	A
31666	Laser Diverter	X	X	X	X	X	X	X	X	A
38200	Laser-Activated Piston	X	X	X	X	X	X	X	X	A
42005	Manually Activated Piston	X	X	X	X	X	X	X	X	A
12834	XS2 Servo Motor		X			X		X	X	B
21032	Manual Servo Motor		X			X		X	X	B
21042	Manual Servo Motor II		X			X		X	X	B
24783	XS3 Servo Motor		X			X		X	X	B
32220	XS4 Servo Motor		X			X		X	X	B
35599	Auto Servo Motor		X	X		X		X	X	B
19283	Photoelectric Detector		X			X		X	X	C
19299	Ionization Detector		X	X		X		X	X	C
23756	Fiber Optic Visual Sensor		X	X	X	X		X	X	C
25030	Radon Detector		X			X		X	X	C
34556	Carbon Monoxide Detector		X		X	X		X	X	C
45890	Motion Detector		X			X		X	X	C

SUMMARY

When developing the product family matrix, we must clearly define what a process is. If parts are not able to run on similar equipment (even if the machine specifications are the same), then we must separate these processes on the product family matrix. If we have a significant number of products, we can sort them by using the logic outlined in Sorting Products on the accompanying CD.

> ## What Have We Done So Far with the EMC Team?
>
> At this point we have explained to the management team:
>
> - ❏ What a product family is
> - ❏ How to create a product family matrix
> - ❏ How to create a product family matrix of EMC Supply's products
> - ❏ How to group their products into families
>
> ## What's Next for the Team?
>
> - ❏ Gather the work content information.
> - ❏ Enter the work content into the product family matrix.
> - ❏ Use work content as criteria for creating product families.

REFINING THE PRODUCT FAMILIES

We can further define product families by using a work content criteria determination. *As a general rule, the total work content of the downstream process steps for each part in the product family should be within 30 percent of each other.* By total work content we mean the total operator time required to build a product as if one person were to perform all of the processing steps. High variations of work content will make it difficult for continuous one-piece flow in a mixed model cell. The result would be a cell or line that pulses quickly on products with short work content, then moves slowly on products with long work content, creating a need to manage and constantly battle potential bottlenecks. It may also require equipment and labor to be added for large work content products, and that means we are back to scheduling the line to use these resources when available, not when the customer wants them.

Obtaining accurate work content for each product can be time consuming. Since we are only using this information to select product families (and not creating standard work with it), we can gather the information by verifying existing information on the shopfloor (a quick check with the operators may speed this along). If products are not running, we may have to use existing standards or estimates. However, if these are not accurate, we will have difficulty balancing the work in the mix (more on this later on pp. 93–107) and may have to redefine our product families.

Defining Product Families

Once the team had collected operator work content time data for each process, they created the following work content matrix for the product family of "Arms & Pistons."

Arms & Pistons Product Family		Hand Deburr	Paint	Weld	Mechanical Assy.	Electrical Assy.	Final Assy.	Configure & Test	Ship	Total
Product Code	**Product Name**									
A	Sensor-Activated Arm	30	60	45	90	140	130	110	X	605
B	Laser-Activated Arm	30	60	30	60	140	100	110	X	530
C	Manually Activated Arm	45	60	40	120	150	90	100	X	605
D	Barcode Diverter Piston	30	60	35	90	180	140	110	X	645
E	Barcode Diverter Arm	60	60	45	100	180	105	105	X	655
F	Sensor-Activated Piston	30	60	40	85	105	90	90	X	500
G	Laser-Activated Piston	30	60	35	150	130	140	200	X	745
H	Manually Activated Piston	30	60	35	80	145	100	100	X	550
I	Laser Diverter	30	60	40	240	300	240	80	X	990
X	Custom Orders	30	60	30	120	160	105	110	X	615

Note—all times are in seconds.

> The team decided that they may need to use hand deburr, which is an alternate process to the machine deburr. The machine deburr requires large batches for optimization. Hand deburr, a bench operation, is a slower process but can be dedicated to a product family. To view the impact of using hand deburr, the team filled in the alternate hand deburr times to see if they affected the total work content.

We can calculate the range of work content by the following formula:

$$\frac{(\text{Highest value} - \text{lowest value})}{\text{Highest value}} \times 100$$

The work content for product I and product G are not within 30 percent of the other products.

We discovered that product I has a much higher total work content than the other products. After more investigation, it was determined that this product could be produced in another area with products that have similar work content. Therefore, it was decided that we could move this product into a different product family.

After moving products around the matrix, the team was able to select a good starting point for a product family. All of the products flowed through the same downstream processing steps. Almost all were within 30 percent of each other for work content, except for product G. Product G was borderline, at 33 per cent. However, there was not another family where it would easily fit. We may revise the product family later based on equipment needs and balancing, but for now we will start this as a family.

The final work content matrix for EMC's product family called Arms & Pistons is shown below.

EMC Supply Company
Work Content Matrix

Product Code	Product Name	Hand Deburr	Paint	Weld	Mechanical Assy.	Electrical Assy.	Final Assy.	Configure & Test	Ship	Total
A	Sensor-Activated Arm	30	60	45	90	140	130	110	X	605
B	Laser-Activated Arm	30	60	30	60	140	100	110	X	530
C	Manually Activated Arm	45	60	40	120	150	90	100	X	605
D	Barcode Diverter Piston	30	60	35	90	180	140	110	X	645
E	Barcode Diverter Arm	60	60	45	100	180	105	105	X	655
F	Sensor-Activated Piston	30	60	40	85	105	90	90	X	500
G	Laser-Activated Piston	30	60	35	150	130	140	200	X	745
H	Manually Activated Piston	30	60	35	80	145	100	100	X	550
X	Custom Orders	30	60	30	120	160	105	110	X	615

Next we headed back to the plant floor with pencil and paper to create a new current-state map of the Arms & Pistons product family. We informed the team that we would first walk through the processing steps for the product family, and then create the process boxes. We would then go back and fill in the data boxes and material flow. Our last step would be to fill in the information flows. The EMC managers had many questions about mapping their more complex environment, so we provided them with a few tips to help.

A Few Mapping Tips

❏ A process can be identified where flow stops and inventory accumulates. For example, two assembly benches may be next to one another; however, 10 pieces of inventory are stacked between the stations. This should be mapped as two process boxes.

❏ For products with multiple parts, identify one part that travels along the main route through the value stream and walk the path as if you were this part. This allows you to start the map with a minimum of complexity.

❏ For products with multiple branches, it might be easier to show only one or two complete branches on your value stream map as you begin. The map might otherwise become complicated very quickly. If possible, map the critical path (the path with the longest lead time—usually it is the one with the most steps).

❏ Do not map only a segment of the value stream. If a value stream is too complex due to multiple branches, select a branch and follow it from beginning to end, then add the other branches later.

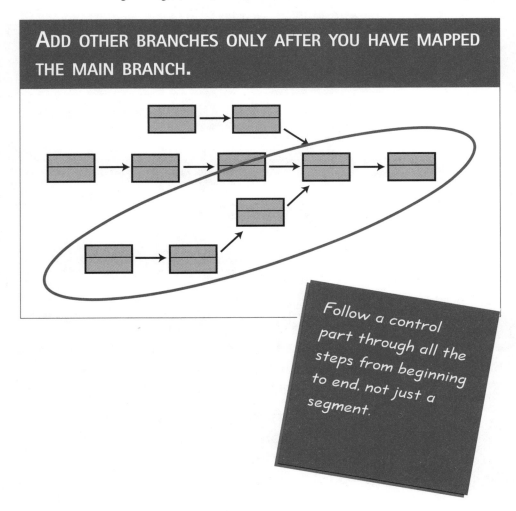

ADD OTHER BRANCHES ONLY AFTER YOU HAVE MAPPED THE MAIN BRANCH.

Follow a control part through all the steps from beginning to end, not just a segment.

❏ To map inventory in front of a shared resource, count *all* of the parts in front of the shared resource (as these may have to be processed first, prior to the part being mapped). Think of a shared resource as the ticket counter at a movie theater. Many people are in line going to see many different movies, but we are only mapping one person going to see a specific movie. The person we are mapping must wait for the people in front of him or her to purchase tickets from the ticket counter (our shared resource), therefore we must account for the time our selected person must stand in line to get through the shared resource. To estimate the wait time at a shared resource (as it may be difficult to get the true demand for all of the parts), use an average cycle time for parts outside the product family, and use the actual demand for the products inside the family.

❏ If a shared resource has many different parts that have been completed and are waiting to be moved, count only the parts within the family, as other parts will follow a different value stream.

❏ Show only one or two main suppliers to start with.

After discussing these tips with the team, we drew upon their knowledge of the products and decided there were three main flows for the product family. We described them as mold, stamp, and paint. We then walked the floor following a main part through each of these flows. We noted the processing steps it required with process boxes on our map. We then added data boxes to record the cycle time, changeover time, uptime, and number of operators. We also indicated any place inventory had accumulated in the flow. We interviewed operators and supervisors to find out how the operators knew what to build next, and then created information flows. Finally, we created a lead-time ladder, which compared total lead time to total processing time. We were able to create a good current-state map based on our observations. This map was as follows (a larger version of the map can be found on the accompanying CD):

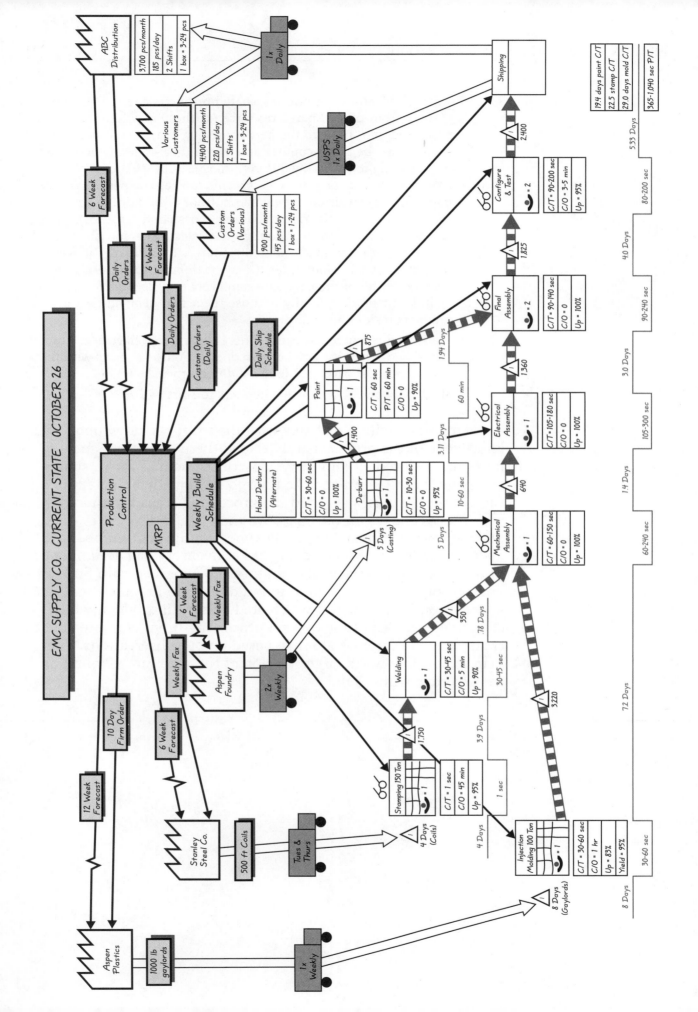

SUMMARY

Developing product families means grouping products that pass through similar downstream processing steps. To further identify product families, we review the total operator work content for each product and target those products that have a total work content within 30 percent of each other. If the operator work content exceeds 30 percent, we should move the product into another product family if possible. If we cannot move it, we may have to leave it in the product family and limit the quantity built at each interval.

What Have We Done So Far with the EMC Team?

- ❏ Taught the management team how to use work content as a criteria to select product families
- ❏ Selected a product family of Arms & Pistons
- ❏ Provided mapping tips to help them develop their current-state map of this product family

What's Next for the Team?

- ❏ Break down the current-state value stream map of the Arms & Pistons product family into loops to reduce the complexity of the entire value stream.
- ❏ Explain how lean principles apply for a high-mix environment in order to develop the future state.

THE CURRENT-STATE MAP

We met back in the conference room to review the current-state map and to be sure it was accurate. The managers stated that their lead time was presently six weeks—roughly what our value stream map showed through our molding flow. We discussed the differences between their first attempt to map and their latest attempt. Understanding and determining the correct product family was very helpful to the team, and their second attempt went much easier than the first. We were now ready to begin the important task of creating a future state with the team.

DEVELOPING A FUTURE STATE

In order to help you follow along with this discussion, we have placed the relevant data in Appendix B: EMC Supply Data Set, pp. 185–188.

Creating the future state was a step-by-step process. To begin, we took the current state and identified resources that could be dedicated (the equipment is portable and inexpensive) in order to create flow (this equipment was named earlier on the product family matrix). We identified shared resources where pull might be needed. We also identified where leveling (creating a schedule for the product family that matches demand as much as possible) would be needed along with a finished-goods policy (the quantity of finished-goods inventory held during different periods of time) to match the leveling. We circled loops on the current-state map to indicate these areas, as shown on p. 45 (a larger version of the map can be found on the accompanying CD). In this manner we could address each area separately, step by step, in order to break down the complexity into manageable bites for future-state development.

The resulting plan to develop the future state was constructed as follows:

Loop 1. Identify resources that can be dedicated to the product family for continuous flow and create a pacemaker process. For the pacemaker, we must answer the following questions:

- ❏ What is takt time?
- ❏ Can our equipment support the takt time?
- ❏ What is the interval?
- ❏ What are the balance charts for the products?
- ❏ How will we balance flow for the mix?
- ❏ How will we create standard work for the mix?

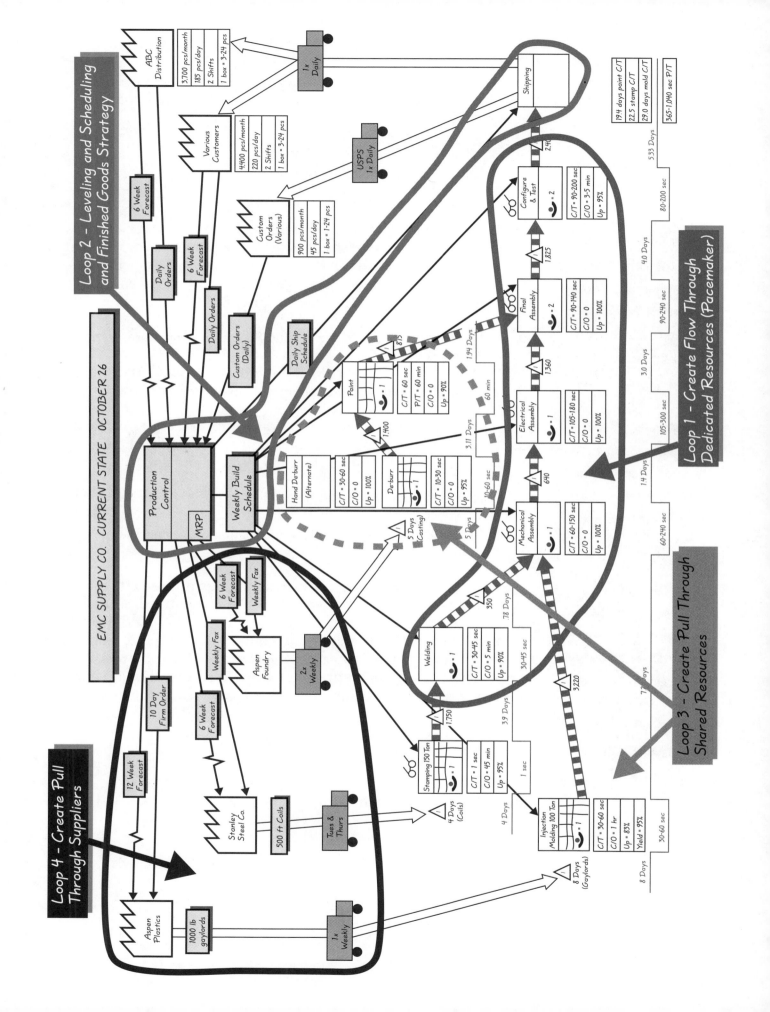

Loop 2. We must decide how we will level the mix if demand is too erratic for the pacemaker. Therefore, we ask:

- ❏ What is the pitch at the pacemaker?
- ❏ How will we schedule the mix at the pacemaker?
- ❏ How will we deal with changes in customer demand?

Loop 3. We will need to identify where a break in flow occurs and create pull through processes outside the pacemaker. For this we need to decide where we can use sequencing with *FIFO (first-in, first-out) lanes* to implement flow upstream from the pacemaker and where shared resources exist. (More on FIFO lanes on p. 50.)

- ❏ Where can we use sequencing and FIFO to link processes to the pacemaker?
- ❏ How will we create pull through the shared resource? How will we signal shared resources to produce the parts needed?

Loop 4. We will need to find suppliers that can react as quickly as our future state can to changes in customer demand. Therefore, we look at the supply side of the value stream and ask:

- ❏ How will we pull work from suppliers so material is delivered only when needed?
- ❏ How will we provide suppliers information to support the changing mix?

It was now time to begin constructing our future-state map. We started with the pacemaker loop. We first identified processes that could be dedicated to the mix of products. We would like to combine these processes and create continuous one-piece flow. Since no inventory will stop *and accumulate,* we illustrate this as one process box on our future-state map. To further develop our pacemaker, we asked further questions about creating flow at these processes. Our first question led us into a lengthy discussion on intervals, takt time, and equipment needs. The age-old question of why shorter intervals are better was discussed heavily.

We have summarized this discussion, as well as determined the first step towards our future state with our next question.

This book will focus on the complexity of a high-mix environment at the critical pacemaker process and will cover, in detail, Loop 1 and Loop 2. The upstream shared-resources and fabrication steps (Loop 3) are pull loops that are used to support the pacemaker. The suppliers of raw material (Loop 4) could also be pull loops or FIFO shipments. These are not covered in this text (see "For Further Reading," p. 190, for titles with additional information.)

THE PACEMAKER LOOP

EMC SUPPLY CO.   FUTURE STATE   PHASE 1 – PACEMAKER   OCTOBER 26

Pacemaker

Mech Assy.   Elec. Assy.   Weld   Final Assy.   Test

Op = ?

Arms & Pistons Customers
450/day
2 Shifts
1 box = 1–24 pcs

UPS
2x daily

Shipping
Stage

6 Week Forecast

Hourly Orders

Daily Ship Schedule

Production Control
MRP
Scheduling

12 Week Forecast

10 Day Firm Order

6 Week Forecast

Weekly Fax

Aspen Foundry
2x Weekly

Stanley Steel Co.
500 ft Coils
Tues & Thurs

Aspen Plastics
1000 lb gaylords
1x Weekly

Paint
C/T = 60 sec
P/T = 60 min
C/O = 0
Up = 90%

Hand Deburr (Alternate)
C/T = 30–60 sec
C/O = 0
Up = 100%

De-Burr
C/T = 10–30 sec
C/O = 0
Up = 95%

Stamping 150 Ton
C/T = 1 sec
C/O = 45 min
Up = 95%

Injection Molding 100 Ton
C/T = 30–60 sec
C/O = 1 hr
Up = 83%
Yield = 95%

5 Days (Casting)
4 Days (Coils)
8 Days (Gaylords)

1,400
1,750
3,220

1.94 Days   60 min   3.11 Days   10–60 sec   5 Days   1 sec   3.9 Days   1 sec   4 Days

QUESTION 2— What Is the Takt Time at the Pacemaker?

One of the lean guidelines is to schedule only one point in the value stream. Work flows downstream from this point to the customer, and before this point we pull from shared resources. The point at which we schedule work is called the *pacemaker*. You can think of the pacemaker as the gas pedal in your car. It sets the rate for how fast the engine will drive the wheels, which in turn determines how fast the car will go. In a lean value stream, the pacemaker determines the speed at which the value stream will operate. The pacemaker will regulate production through the value stream. Increasing the speed of the pacemaker should result in more products being produced through the value stream. Slowing down the pacemaker means that fewer products will be produced.

To create a pacemaker, we dedicate equipment (such as hand assembly benches, power-assisted assembly, and small presses) to run the specified family. This equipment is moved together to form a cell or line through which parts continuously flow, one piece at a time, without stoppage.

We may also be able to separate equipment used for shared resources into product families. This can be done by determining how much machine time is needed just to support a product family. If we can move the shared resource work needed for a product family onto specific machines and dedicate them, we can truly eliminate the spaghetti flow from our shopfloor!

Sometimes processes must be separated due to distance or imbalance of cycle times. We can still use flow thorugh the use of a FIFO (first-in, first-out) lane. The FIFO lane keeps the sequence of the production uniform throughout the value stream and maintains flow. FIFO lanes do hold inventory, so we want to make sure they are not too big, otherwise they just become storage areas.

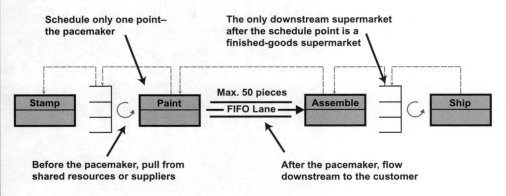

At EMC Supply, we realized that while we can flow through the paint process, it will be shared with other product families. Therefore, we cannot have it dedicated to the Arms & Pistons product family. Since hand deburr happens before paint, we could not include this process in our pacemaker either. Therefore, our pacemaker will be comprised of welding, mechanical assembly, electrical assembly, final assembly, and testing. We must balance each of these processes to a constant speed in order to create flow. The best speed to balance (the one that provides the least amount of waste) is called *takt time*.

TAKT TIME

Takt time is the customer demand rate. It is used to synchronize the pace of production with the pace of sales, particularly at the pacemaker process. It guides us, telling us how quickly we should produce. In mixed model production, takt is calculated at the pacemaker by dividing the effective working time by the total demand for all the various models running through the pacemaker:

$$\text{Takt} = \frac{\text{Effective working time}}{\text{Sum (Demand during that time)}}$$

Effective working time is the available work time minus breaks and lunches. Do not subtract downtime, setup time, maintenance, and other interruptions, or you will get a false sense of the rate of customer demand.

Takt time is the customer demand rate. It can be thought of as a mighty metronome running in the factory. Just as a metronome is used to keep a constant rhythm or beat in music, here it sets the rhythm of customer demand. A typical unit of measure is minutes or seconds; sometimes it may be hours or days.

One helpful way to calculate demand is to review the actual customer shipments of a recent time period. This is rarely the same as forecast or as the current production rate.

It may be helpful to add a demand column to your product family matrix (PFM) with the work content. EMC's PFM, with the demand column added, is shown below.

Product Code	Product Name	Weld	Mechanical Assy.	Electrical Assy.	Final Assy.	Configure & Test	Ship	Total Work Content	Demand/Week	Demand/Day
A	Sensor-Activated Arm	45	90	140	130	110	X	515	325	65
B	Laser-Activated Arm	30	60	140	100	110	X	440	425	85
C	Manually Activated Arm	40	120	150	90	100	X	500	175	35
D	Barcode Diverter Piston	35	90	180	140	110	X	555	350	70
E	Barcode Diverter Arm	45	100	180	105	105	X	535	250	50
F	Sensor-Activated Piston	40	85	105	90	90	X	410	275	55
G	Laser-Activated Piston	35	150	130	140	200	X	655	100	20
H	Manually Activated Piston	35	80	145	100	100	X	460	125	25
X	Custom Orders	30	120	160	105	110	X	540	225	45
									2250	450

Arms & Pistons Product Family

In EMC's case, the total demand for parts in assembly is 2,025 units per week of eight different products. We also allowed for 225 custom products to be built per week. This gives us a total demand of 2,250 units per week.

Takt time could be calculated off of the weekly number, but if possible, we want to think smaller. We calculated based on a daily demand of 450 units per day.

The effective working time in assembly is 450 minutes (480 minutes–30 minutes for breaks) per shift $\times$ 2 shifts. This yields an effective working time of 900 minutes per shift.

Effective working time (hours) = (8—[2 × 0.25]) × 2 = 15 hours

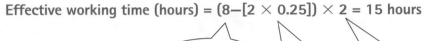

Hours/day

2 breaks/ shift

2 shifts

Effective working time/day (minutes) = 15 hours × 60 = 900 minutes

As a result, the takt time is equal to two minutes:

$$\text{Takt} = \frac{900 \text{ minutes}}{450 \text{ units}} = 2 \text{ minutes (or 120 seconds)}$$

This is the average takt time for this product family. In other words, customers are currently buying products from the Arms & Pistons product family at the rate of one every two minutes. At what rate we will actually assemble these products (the "planned cycle time") will be discussed later on pp. 78–79.

When grouping products we need to understand the nature of the takt time that will be created by the mix. In general, when takt falls below 10 seconds the work becomes highly repetitive, and it is hard to develop a suitable rotation of duties in a continuous flow environment (which also helps eliminate repetitive strain ergonomic issues). When this situation occurs, you need to determine whether products can be removed from this product family and moved to another. This will reduce the demand on the product family and increase the takt time. When takt exceeds 5 minutes, the number of elements each operator has to perform makes it difficult to insure cycle time and consistency. Standard work (which we will discuss later, pp. 109–114) becomes critical to drive out variability. Here, you may consider adding products to the cell as this increases volume and reduces takt time. This, in turn, will reduce the number of elements each operator has to perform, and should drive out the variability in end cycle times.

There are also times when two or more product families go through one manual assembly cell (area of continuous one-piece flow). In this case we can break the cell into separate cells to create individual dedicated pacemakers.

SUMMARY

Once a current-state value stream map has been created, our next step is to create a future-state value stream map. This future-state map will clearly show which process will drive the pace or heartbeat of the value stream. We identify this process as the pacemaker. The pacemaker process must have the equipment required dedicated to the product family. A shared resource cannot easily be a pacemaker for a product family. The pacemaker usually is in the form of a cell (an area where continuous one-piece flow exists). The pacemaker is also the only point where we schedule the value stream. After this point we flow downstream to customers. Before this point, we pull from shared resources or suppliers.

What Have We Done So Far with the EMC Team?

Back in the conference room, we found that the discussion had gone well. The team seemed to understand product families and takt. So far we have discussed with them:

- ❒ Identifying the pacemaker process.
- ❒ Establishing takt time for the pacemaker process.

We illustrated the pacemaker on the whiteboard. Below the pacemaker we added our data box to record the information needed for the pacemaker to support the value stream.

What's Next for the Team?

Our next task with the team is to:

- ❒ Determine if our machines can support the takt time at the pacemaker.

We will next need to review the equipment used at the pacemaker to make sure we have the right amount of equipment in place for the product mix that will occur.

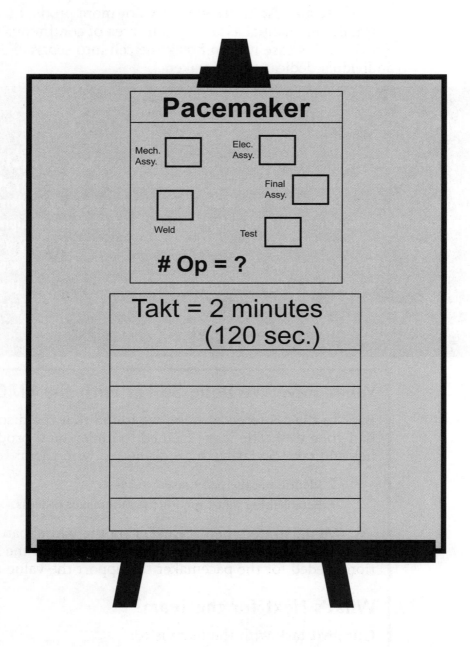

QUESTION 3—
Can the Equipment Support the Takt Time?

Since machine cycles (the actual time the machine requires to perform its work) may be fixed and not easily changed, we should perform a quick check to ensure we have enough machine capacity to support the proposed product family and mix within the takt time. Labor time is flexible, as we can periodically add or subtract people from a cell or line. We will look at the labor needs later when we develop the cell for flow, pp. 100–104.

At EMC Supply, the pacemaker consists mostly of electro-mechanical assembly, with machines being used for spot-welding and testing. Since spot-welding has a very small machine cycle (less than two seconds) compared to the cycle time, we can skip this piece of equipment for our analysis. Therefore, we will perform equipment analysis on the testing equipment. At the test station, products are attached to a tester by the operator, then run for a specified fixed test cycle to complete the test. The operator must observe the diagnostic screen while the test is running and cannot leave the station until the test cycle is complete. Each product has a different test cycle.

To determine the test equipment needs, we will need to know effective working hours, along with the cycle time of each product at the testing process.

CYCLE TIME

By cycle time we mean the frequency at which we get a piece out of a process (as if we were catching one each time it came out of the process). We could also define it as the time it takes an operator to go through all of his or her work elements before repeating them.

Cycle Times for Testing

Product Code	Product Name	Cycle Time (C/T)	Demand (per day)	C/T x Demand
A	Sensor-Activated Arm	110 sec	65	7150 sec
B	Laser-Activated Arm	110 sec	85	9350 sec
C	Manually Activated Arm	100 sec	35	3500 sec
D	Barcode Diverter Piston	110 sec	70	7700 sec
E	Barcode Diverter Arm	105 sec	50	5250 sec
F	Sensor-Activated Piston	90 sec	55	4950 sec
G	Laser-Activated Piston	200 sec	20	4000 sec
H	Manually Activated Piston	100 sec	25	2500 sec
X	Custom Orders	110 sec	45	4950 sec
Sum (C/T x Demand) or Time Needed = 49,350 seconds				

To determine the number of machines required at the testing process, we divide the machine time needed by the effective working time.

Equipment required =
Sum (C/T x Demand)/Effective working time

or

$$\text{Equipment required} = \frac{\text{Time needed}}{\text{Effective working time}} = \frac{49,350}{54,000} = .91 \text{ machines}$$

We can use the product family matrix to calculate the resources required for a process, as follows.

Arms & Pistons Product Family		Configure & Test	Demand/Week	Testing time
Product Code	Product Name			
A	Sensor-Activated Arm	110	65	7150
B	Laser-Activated Arm	110	85	9350
C	Manually Activated Arm	100	35	3500
D	Barcode Diverter Piston	110	70	7700
E	Barcode Diverter Arm	105	50	5250
F	Sensor-Activated Piston	90	55	4950
G	Laser-Activated Piston	200	20	4000
H	Manually Activated Piston	100	25	2500
X	Custom Orders	110	45	4950
			TIME NEEDED	49350
		Effective Working Time = 54000 sec		54000
			MACHINES REQUIRED	0.91

We may also have to consider uptime. Uptime is the amount of time the machine is in good working order when you need it. It may be thought of as the opposite of downtime. The testing stations currently have an uptime of 95 percent, which means that the testing machines tend to break down about 5 percent of the time. Thus, we may have to add more time to cover the time lost for breakdowns if we do not fix the uptime issues. Let's see the impact of uptime by increasing the time needed.

$$\text{Total time needed} = \frac{49{,}350}{.95 \text{ uptime}} = 51{,}947 \text{ seconds}$$

or

$$\text{Equipment required} = \frac{\text{Total time needed}}{\text{Effective working time}} = \frac{51{,}947}{54{,}000} = .96 \text{ machines!}$$

It is important that uptime not be buried in the equipment calculation. Instead we choose to see the impact of uptime so it can be focused upon and improved. In this case, with uptime improvement we may be able to support the mix with only one machine, and not have to purchase a second tester.

This means that we will need one tester dedicated to this product family at all times. In fact, with the current uptime, one tester is probably not enough! With the current loading of 96 percent (total time needed/total effective working time) it looks like the testers won't be able to miss a beat! The uptime of 95 percent will have to be improved to allow for mix fluctuations that will occur. We may wish to look for another tester that can cycle faster, or reduce the test cycle times through process improvement. This also indicates that we may have to *level the mix* to insure certain mixes do not exceed testing capacity. We will discuss leveling the mix later in this book on pp. 144–146.

Custom Products in the Same Value Stream

Custom products are also a part of the Arms & Pistons product family, and EMC Supply Company processes these parts through the same value stream. Therefore, we must allow time in our equipment calculations for custom products. At this point we put in an estimated cycle time in a product named "custom." We could also reduce the machine loading to allow time for custom products based on their percentage of the mix. At EMC Supply, custom products are expected to be 10 percent (45 units per day out of 450 units total) of the mix, so we reduce the machine loading by an estimated 10 percent to a target of 70 to 75 percent. We know this will change on a day-to-day basis, so we will check the mix each day to see how much time is available for custom products. We will discuss how to check the mix on a daily basis in detail on pp. 141–144.

As a starting point, we may target a resource requirement of 80 to 85 percent, not to allow all of the remaining time for setups but to allow for variations in the mix at each interval. It should be noted that this is not a machine utilization number, because machine utilization is a dynamic number that tries to measure the shopfloor performance and leads us away from lean practices. This is merely a resource calculation. We also use 80 to 85 percent to allow for product growth, as we hope you are growing!

SUMMARY

Once we identify the pacemaker and establish takt time, we need to determine if the machines used at the pacemaker can support the taxt time for the mix of products. We may need to add equipment to support the mix, or level the mix if we are restricted on the amount of equipment available. We should also consider the uptime of the equipment as this can impact its ability to support takt time. The cost of fixing poor uptime may offset the cost of buying new equipment, and prove to be a worthwhile investment.

What Have We Done So Far with the EMC Team?

In this section we have led the EMC management team in determining the equipment required to support the takt time. This included:

- ❏ Defining cycle times
- ❏ Calculating total time needed by machine
- ❏ Determining the number of machines needed
- ❏ Considering the impact of uptime

The management team has asked many questions that tell us they are eager to learn more. In fact, they are ready to create a pacemaker and begin moving machines right now! We congratulated them on their willingness to take action, as this is key to a lean implementation. However, there are still a few things to think about before we start moving equipment.

What's Next for the Team?

Our next task with the team is to determine the time interval that will enable them to cycle through every product in the family. This will include:

- ❏ The number of changeovers that can be performed
- ❏ Changeover time needed to support the interval
- ❏ Determining the smallest lot size possible

The interval concept is a key concept and measurement in the value stream. It should be used to monitor value stream performance and improvement. It can also be a challenging concept to explain, so we plan to spend some time on it and lay it out with some illustrations. Everyone on the management team must fully understand the concept of the interval, as it gets right to the heart of people's preconception about batches being better.

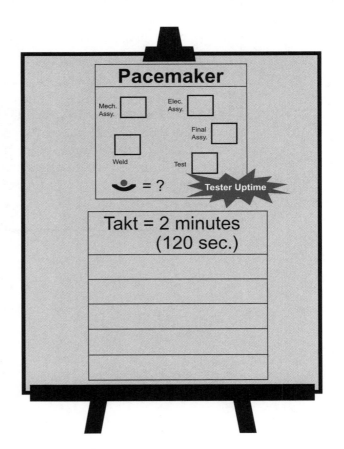

QUESTION 4—
What Is the Interval?

The concept of *the interval* is key in applying lean thinking. In mixed model production the concept of the interval plays a much stronger role. It is essential not only that we fully understand this concept, but that the people on the shopfloor talk in terms of the interval when discussing the progress of their lean implementation. In fact, the length of the current interval should be a key metric to measure progress in their lean journey.

When we ask "What is the interval?," we are asking, "At what time interval will you be able to run through every regular product in the family?" Every week? Every two days? Every shift? If a company assembles a part once per month, how much do they have to make when they run it? Well, they would have to make a month's worth. If they can assemble the product each day, they can just make a day's worth. That's how the interval works. It's really a measure of your batch size, and we all know that smaller is better. Sometimes the interval is known as *EPEI*[1], which stands for *every part every interval*—in short, how long will it take (what time interval) to produce every part in the family?

---

1. *Learning to See (Version 1.2)*. Mike Rother and John Shook. The Lean Enterprise Institute, 1999, p. 54.

Some product families contain a high number of products in the family, but only a certain percentage of them are actively made. In this case we could consider the EPEI to be the *ability to produce* so many part numbers over a certain period of time. Remember—we only want to build what the customer orders each day.

OBTAINING SHORT INTERVALS MEANS LEVELING THE MIX OF PRODUCTS THAT WILL RUN THROUGH THE PACEMAKER. CAN WE RUN THE MIX ONCE PER WEEK? ONCE PER DAY?

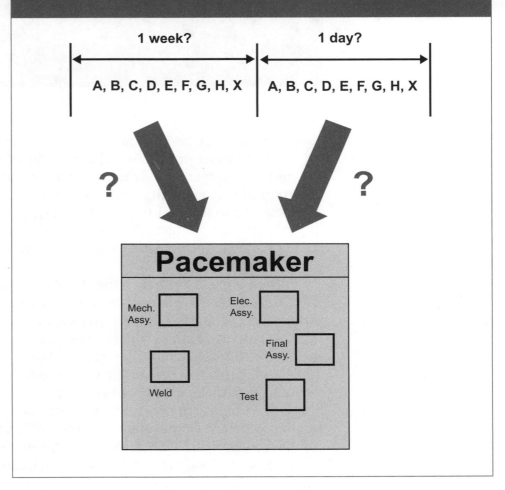

Let's illustrate the concept of the interval. The customer's weekly demand is as follows.

Product Code		Weekly Demand
A	Sensor-Activated Arm	325
B	Laser-Activated Arm	425
C	Manually Activated Arm	175
D	Barcode Diverter Piston	350
E	Barcode Diverter Arm	250
F	Sensor-Activated Piston	275
G	Laser-Activated Piston	100
H	Manually Activated Piston	125
X	Custom Orders	225
	TOTAL	2250

Daily production must equal 450 units to meet this demand, but how will we schedule it? It would seem efficient to set the interval to one week and schedule as follows.

Product Code	Product Name	Monday	Tuesday	Wednesday	Thursday	Friday
A	Sensor-Activated Arm	325				
B	Laser-Activated Arm	125	300			
C	Manually Activated Arm		150	25		
D	Barcode Diverter Piston			350		
E	Barcode Diverter Arm			75	175	
F	Sensor-Activated Piston				275	
G	Laser-Activated Piston					100
H	Manually Activated Piston					125
X	Custom Orders					225
	TOTAL	450	450	450	450	450

← —————————— Interval = 1 week —————————— →

It would be better still if we could achieve an interval of one day and produce these orders as follows.

Product Code	Product Name	Monday	Tuesday	Wednesday	Thursday	Friday
A	Sensor-Activated Arm	65	65	65	65	65
B	Laser-Activated Arm	85	85	85	85	85
C	Manually Activated Arm	35	35	35	35	35
D	Barcode Diverter Piston	70	70	70	70	70
E	Barcode Diverter Arm	50	50	50	50	50
F	Sensor-Activated Piston	55	55	55	55	55
G	Laser-Activated Piston	20	20	20	20	20
H	Manually Activated Piston	25	25	25	25	25
X	Custom Orders	45	45	45	45	45
	TOTAL	450	450	450	450	450

Interval = 1 day

> Producing in small intervals requires very quick changeover times and high machine reliability. We must constantly reduce changeover times to reduce the interval!

Creating small intervals to run the mix of products is key to the success of a mixed model line. As intervals shrink, good things happen. Flexibility is dramatically increased, on-time delivery to customers increases, changeover times become very small, and inventory is almost nonexistent. When intervals really get small (say under a shift) then the shopfloor has become the "race car pit crew" of manufacturing—*not a bad thing to have in your factory!*

This is a good time to look at the Chaos Graph we used earlier. We can explain that smaller intervals mean smaller lead time. Therefore, the amount of chaos is directly related to EPEI, in the same manner.

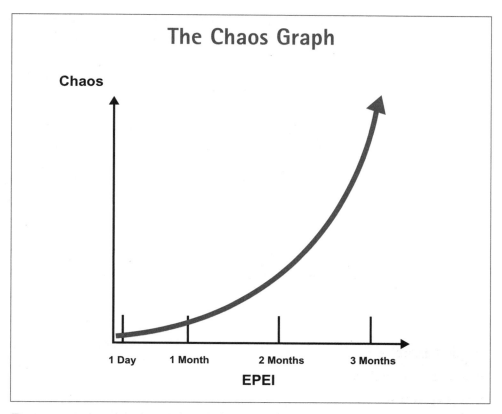

DETERMINING THE INTERVAL

Working out the interval is not a one-time calculation, unless you are in a company that has a very stable demand from the customer on a regular basis. It is a balancing act of matching demand, available equipment resources, cycle times, and work hours. As continuous improvement activities take place and waste is eliminated (setup times, downtime, etc.), the interval can be reduced.

Selecting the interval is not an exact science—it is an iterative process. We will follow guidelines to determine a starting point (estimated interval), then go back and tune in on the right interval. The guidelines for selecting the interval are:

1. Select a starting point for the interval based on how long you think it will take to cycle through all of the products in the family based on the number of changeovers you can do per day (covered below).

2. Determine if you have enough equipment to support the interval.

3. Design the flow of work through the pacemaker. (See Part III, "Flow at the Pacemaker.")

4. If the assumed interval cannot be met (due to changeovers or work-flow) or can be reduced, estimate a new interval and repeat steps 2 and 3.

5. If a reasonable interval cannot be met, you may have to revise the product families and repeat steps 1 to 4 (see page 70).

To begin, try to select an interval that is close to your current EPEI. For example, if you feel you could currently cycle through every part in the family every week, select an interval of one week. If you feel it takes about a month to run all the products, start with one month. There will be times when it seems it might take a year to run all the products in the family, as demand for some products is very low. In this case, use the 80/20 rule and decide how long it currently takes to run the majority (or 80 percent) of the products in the family. Another way to think of your current interval is to pick a steady product in the family and ask, "How often do I run this product?"

A good exercise would be to analyze whether you have enough capacity to make every part every day, or even better—every time a truck leaves the building! This is called the "every part every ship window," and it can turn your factory into a money pump!

Another approach is to select a target interval such as one day as a starting point. This target may seem unattainable, but it gets people thinking in the right direction.

An aggressive approach is to select as a starting interval the rate at which you currently ship to your customers—*this tends to show how much waste needs to be eliminated!*

EMC had been issuing weekly schedules. They felt their interval was approximately one week. We wanted to get them thinking what lean could do for them quickly, so we used a starting interval of one day. Since EMC ships to their customers daily, this will provide them with the vision that they may be able to build and ship what their customers want each and every day!

Now we can determine the changeover time needed to support the interval. A simple changeover graph[2] can help us explain how this is done.

---

2. *Learning to See (Version 1.2)*. Mike Rother and John Shook. The Lean Enterprise Institute, 1999 p. 54.

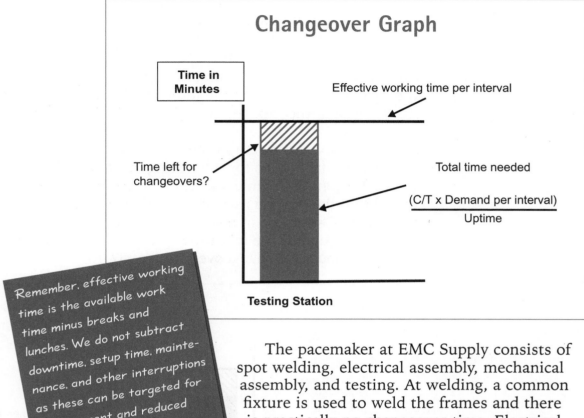

Changeover Graph

Time in Minutes

Effective working time per interval

Time left for changeovers?

Total time needed

$$\frac{(C/T \times \text{Demand per interval})}{\text{Uptime}}$$

Testing Station

Remember, effective working time is the available work time minus breaks and lunches. We do not subtract downtime, setup time, maintenance, and other interruptions as these can be targeted for improvement and reduced or eliminated.

The pacemaker at EMC Supply consists of spot welding, electrical assembly, mechanical assembly, and testing. At welding, a common fixture is used to weld the frames and there is practically no changeover time. Electrical and mechanical assembly use generic tables and can be changed over in 1 to 2 minutes. The real challenge is the test equipment. Currently the changeover times at testing are 3 to 5 minutes. Therefore, we will focus our interval calculation at the testing station, to see what interval it can support.

First we need to determine the effective working time for the testing machines. This was calculated previously to be 900 minutes in the "Takt Time" section (pp. 50–54).

$$\frac{\text{Effective working}}{\text{time/day (minutes)}} = 15 \text{ hours} \times 60 = 900 \text{ minutes}$$

Note: Configure and Test will run two shifts for 8 hours/shift with two 15-minute breaks.

$$\frac{\text{Effective working}}{\text{time/day (seconds)}} = 900 \text{ minutes} \times 60 = 54{,}000 \text{ seconds}$$

As we mentioned earlier, the changeover times on the test station are 3 to 5 minutes. However, we did not use the existing setup times. Instead, we asked: "What setup times are needed to support the interval?" If the setup times for a particular mix cannot be met, we look again at reducing setup times, reducing the cycle time, increasing the interval, changing the product family, or leveling the mix, as we will discuss later (on pp. 144–146).

Let's look at the setup time needed at the testing station. The effective available time for the testing machine is 900 minutes (54,000 seconds) per interval. The uptime for the tester is 95 percent. From the previous section we learned that we need 866 minutes (51,947 seconds) of test time (including the 95 percent uptime) to support the takt time each day. That leaves 34 minutes (2,053 seconds) for changeovers (see p. 57).

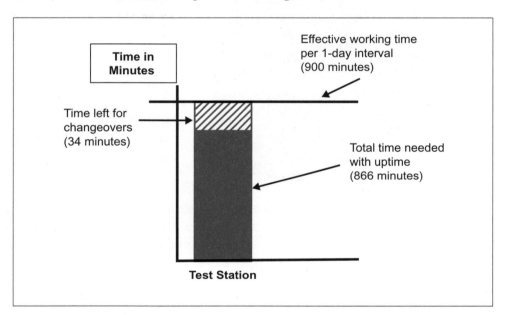

If we assemble each product once per day, we'll need to go through nine changeovers.

$$\frac{34 \text{ minutes}}{9 \text{ products}} = 3.8 \text{ minutes maximum changeover time}$$

The current changeovers are 3 to 5 minutes, and our interval will only allow 3.8 minutes per changeover. We need to improve the current changeover times. We could probably work on the few part numbers that are over 3.8 minutes and easily get all part numbers under 3.8 minutes. Should we go further than this? We know that building in smaller increments provides even more flexibility, discipline, reduced chaos, and perhaps increased market share (if we offer to ship to customers twice per day, will we get more business?). If we could improve the uptime to 98 percent and reduce changeover time to 3 minutes or less, we could produce each product two times per day (once per shift) *and run even smaller lots through the pacemaker!* This would allow us to level and spread the mix throughout two shifts, which will also help reduce large lots being made at the shared resources. Therefore, *we will target an uptime of 98 percent and an interval of one shift,* and list the necessary kaizen activities to achieve this in our future state.

SHOULD WE WORK ON UPTIME?

We can perform a quick calculation to determine the impact of uptime (machine reliability) on changeovers. With an uptime of 100 percent, we would have 77.5 minutes (54,000 seconds, or 900 minutes — 49,350 seconds, or 822.5 minutes) available for changeovers. If we could improve each changeover to less than 2 minutes, we could change our interval to 4 times per day! (9 products $\times$ 2 minutes/changeover = 18 minutes in C/O. 77.5 minutes available/ 18 minutes in changeover = 4.3).

What If We Can't Reduce Uptime or Changeovers Quickly?

One method is to work overtime to make up for the lost time. We would have to add time between the shifts so each shift could work a little longer. Adding overtime makes the downtime visual and expensive, allowing everyone to see just how much it really costs. This in turn helps focus attention on strategies to eliminate the cost of overtime.

Another method to recover from lost time is to temporarily build bigger batches by increasing the interval. This allows for more interruptions, as less changeover time is needed. Make sure this is only a temporary solution, because *increasing the interval decreases flexibility to respond to the customer.*

If the interval cannot be supported, we have a few options:

1. Reduce the changeover time of the equipment.

2. Reduce the cycle time of the equipment.

3. Improve the uptime of the equipment.

4. Produce parts on alternate processes.

5. Work extra hours (overtime).

6. Add an additional shift.

7. Buy extra equipment.

8. Redefine the product family by adding or removing products.

9. Build bigger batches (for now) by increasing the interval.

SUMMARY

The interval is a key concept in mixed model production. The interval tells us how long it will take to cycle through all the products in the family. Shorter intervals are always better. The interval is also a measure of batch size and flexibility. The smaller the batch size, the more flexible we become. Having small intervals allows the most flexibility to build what the customers want, when they want it.

The interval is not a one-time calculation. We may revise and perform the interval calculation often to determine if our machines can support the interval. We must be cautious and ask "What setup times are needed to support the interval?," not "What is the interval based on our current setup times?" Asking the latter would only bury into our value stream waste that would never be eliminated.

What Have We Done So Far with the EMC Team?

We have explained to the team the concept and importance of the interval, including:

- ❏ Why smaller intervals are better
- ❏ How to determine an interval
- ❏ How to calculate the time available for changeovers
- ❏ How to determine a target changeover time to support the selected interval

We have determined that EMC Supply can support an interval of one shift by improving uptime to 98 percent and reducing changeover time to less than three minutes.

It was commonly thought at EMC that large intervals (yielding larger lot sizes) were more efficient, as they reduced lengthy changeovers. The concept of the interval began to dissuade them from this concept and point them toward transforming their culture to a lean one. This proved pivotal in getting the organization moving in the right direction.

What's Next for the Team?

Our next step is to teach the management team:

- ❏ How to balance flow for the pacemaker
- ❏ The use of balance charts for the product family
- ❏ Methods for balancing various cycle times

We will review some concepts on balancing and introduce a few new concepts in order to handle balancing the mix in their environment. We will then apply some new techniques at the pacemaker to sustain flow through the various mixes. The managers were familiar with the basic concepts of cell design, which was essential before proceeding.

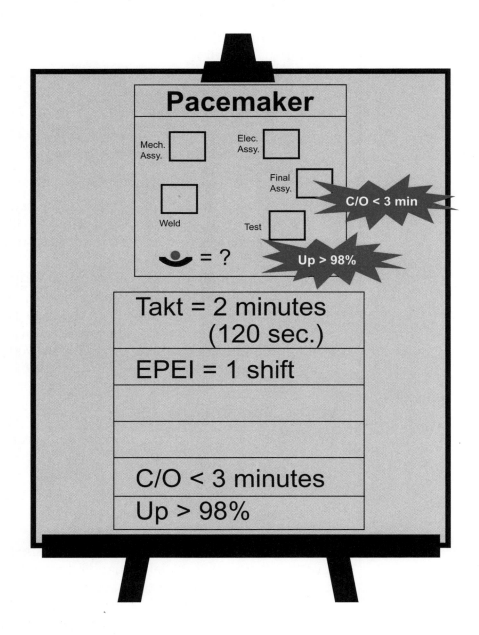

PART III:
FLOW AT THE PACEMAKER

- ❏ Question 5—What Are the Operator Balance Charts for the Products?

- ❏ Question 6—How Will We Balance Flow for the Mix?

- ❏ Question 7—How Will We Create Standard Work for the Mix?

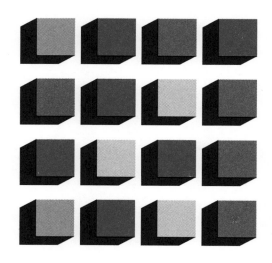

QUESTION 5—

What Are the Operator Balance Charts for the Products?

In mixed model manufacturing, the best situation is to have every product in the mix be balanced to a cycle time close to the takt time at each station. If this were the case (and we should strive to obtain this situation) it would not matter which product the customer ordered. All products could be made in the same amount of time, at the same rate, using the same number of people. All products would "march" through the cell at the same rate.

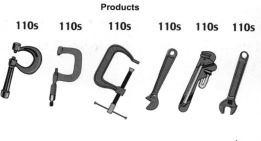

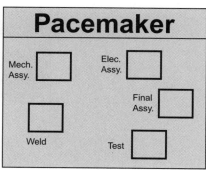

However, this may not occur due to the work content for some products, making them difficult to balance with others. Remember, we try to group products that are within 30 percent of each other in terms of work content. With more than this variation, some products may exceed the takt time needed. Some may also have machine cycles that are fixed, which may cause them to exceed takt time. A process that cannot meet takt time is called a *bottleneck*.

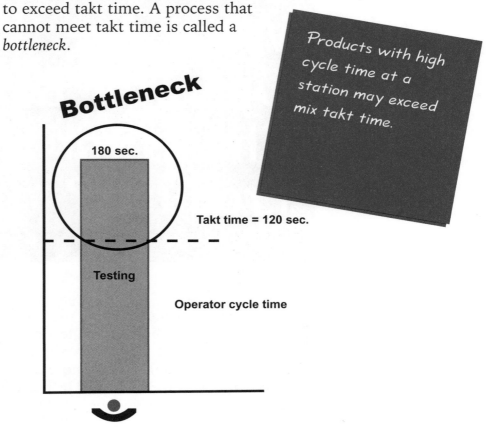

Products with high cycle time at a station may exceed mix takt time.

Bottleneck

180 sec.

Takt time = 120 sec.

Testing

Operator cycle time

The testing station might be a bottleneck for one or two products in the family. The others might be okay. Later we will see why (see p. 87).

One method for balancing work for flow is to use an operator balance chart (OBC). This tool helps us balance work content per operator to takt time and, as a result, create continuous one-piece flow between operators at the pacemaker.

An operator balance chart looks like a bar chart or a histogram. It displays the number of operators and the work content time for each. OBC's are created for the current state and the future state. In the current state we show the existing times for each product at each operation. From the current state we try to rebalance the products in the family so they flow through at the same rate, no matter what the product (see the example that follows).

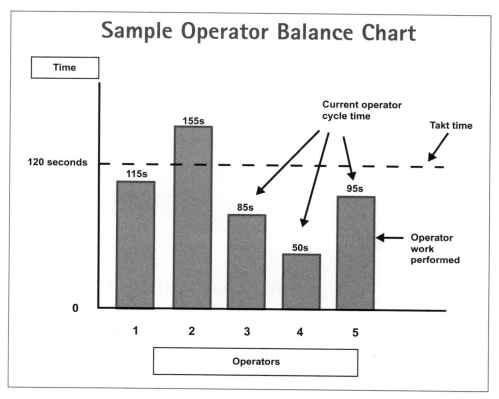

If the products cannot be exactly balanced due to different work content, we load all except the last operator to takt time and allow the waste to show at the last station. Following this method we can target to remove the waste and the last station. We would then demonstrate our new balance in the future-state OBC (see the example on the next page).

In mixed production, we need to create operator balance charts for each product in the family to understand the work that needs to be performed at each station for each product. Workstations must be flexible, as different products may require different processes to be performed at the same workstation. These balance charts will also show how work will be distributed for high work content products, and where to target potential areas of improvement for better balancing.

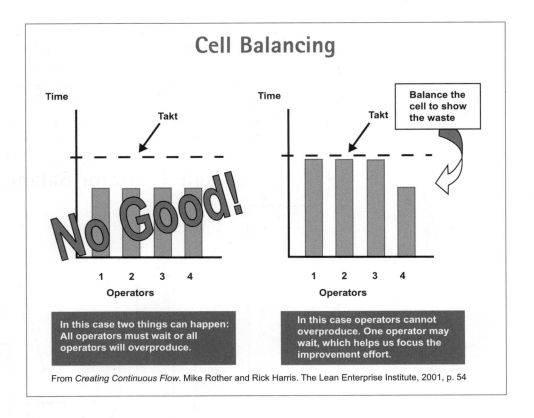

Cell Balancing

Time — Takt

No Good!

1 2 3 4
Operators

In this case two things can happen: All operators must wait or all operators will overproduce.

Time — Takt

Balance the cell to show the waste

1 2 3 4
Operators

In this case operators cannot overproduce. One operator may wait, which helps us focus the improvement effort.

From *Creating Continuous Flow*. Mike Rother and Rick Harris. The Lean Enterprise Institute, 2001, p. 54

WHAT TIME DO WE BALANCE TO?

- Takt = the customer demand rate
- Planned cycle time = the rate we produce at to meet customer demand

Takt is the customer demand rate. If we balance the workstations at takt time, then any variation (longer cycle time, scrap, rework, different operator) will cause us to not make takt time and be short on customer orders. We often carry inventory to buffer against these variations. We can also counter these variations by balancing the work at each station slightly faster than takt time. This is called the *planned cycle time (PCT)*. A good target for the planned cycle time is around 92 to 95 percent of takt. This percentage allows for operator fatigue, minor interruptions in the cycle, and the variation of work content between products. Variations such as downtime, setup, and scrap are not included in the planned cycle time, as we do not want to bury these variations, we want to eliminate them. We allow for these variations, as we did with uptime, in determining the equipment needs.

To overcome variations, we can use a method that we mentioned earlier. We can balance close to takt time and use overtime to make up for the time lost due to variation. This will really make the variations stand out and focus attention on getting them reduced quickly!

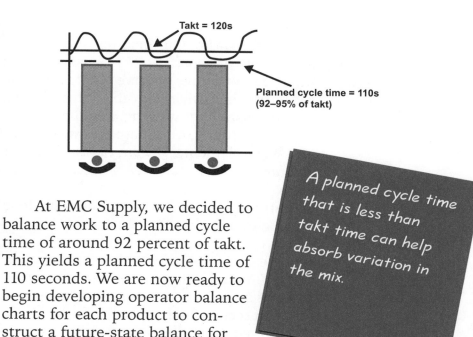

A planned cycle time that is less than takt time can help absorb variation in the mix.

At EMC Supply, we decided to balance work to a planned cycle time of around 92 percent of takt. This yields a planned cycle time of 110 seconds. We are now ready to begin developing operator balance charts for each product to construct a future-state balance for the mix of products.

CREATING OPERATOR BALANCE CHARTS

To develop the balance charts, we need to gather the work content data at each station. Of course, the best place to do this is out on the shopfloor. When observing the operator, it is important not to include any obvious waste such as walking, getting tools that are not located in a specific position, and extra inspection (this is another good reason not to use engineering standards, as these are often not accurate and include waste). For example, when we arrived at the welding station and observed the operator, he performed the following activities.

The operator gathered a part from a bin and loaded it into a fixture. He then secured the fixture in four places by hand turning wheels with handles. The operator then lined up the electrode to the part and double-checked its placement. He lowered a welding shield and then activated the press. The welding cycle was complete in less than two seconds. The operator lifted the shield, then loosened the fixture with the four wheels. He inspected the part, placed it on a carrying tray, and then walked to place it aside.

At first the team timed the entire cycle from the operator picking up a part to weld until he put it down after welding, but we asked them a question: *Is there any waste in this operation?*

They observed the operator again and realized that many of the tasks were waste. Our next question was: *"Should we include this waste in our balance charts?"* They answered no. We then instructed them that when we observe work, we should not include any waste that is easily removable. This waste may be in the form of material handling, walking, bending, overprocessing, and other waste. In order to eliminate this waste, we break down the work into work elements. *A work element is the smallest increment of work that can be moved to another operator.*[1] Since we don't know where the work will be split and moved to another operator, we use this definition to insure the work could be done by another operator at the end of any element.

We then broke down the welding operation by work elements and did not record the elements of walking and getting parts from bins. There was the further waste of turning the four wheels many times to secure the fixture. While we knew these could be eliminated, it could not be done quickly, as a new fixture would need to be designed and built. Therefore, we left this in and identified it for future improvements.

The team recorded the elements several times and obtained various readings. When we were asked: "Which time should we use?," we simply replied: "What is the lowest repeatable time?"

We next went to the testing station. The operator must run a diagnostic test and monitor the machine during the cycle. It was difficult to determine what elements of work could be passed on to the next operator during the test cycle. In fact, we found that none of it could. We realized that testing would require one operator dedicated to the tester, as he or she would be unable to move to another station or have another operator take over during the test cycle.

Once we instructed the team on how to gather the data, they were off and running. It took some time, but the team received some assistance from the operators, expediting the task. Once they were done, we reconvened in the conference room to review the data and build the balance charts, which are shown on the next few pages.

---

1. *Creating Continuous Flow*. Mike Rother and Rick Harris. The Lean Enterprise Institute, 2001, p. 17.

Current State

Operator Balance Chart—Part A
(Sensor-Activated Arm)

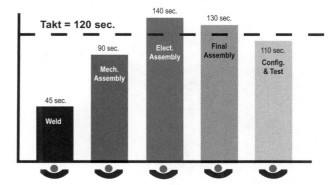

Operator Balance Chart—Part B
(Laser-Activated Arm)

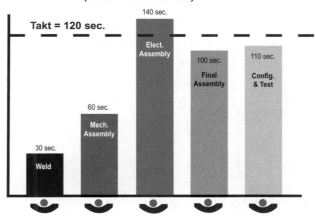

Operator Balance Chart—Part C
(Manually Activated Arm)

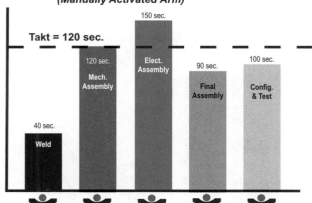

Future State

Operator Balance Chart—Part A
(Sensor-Activated Arm)

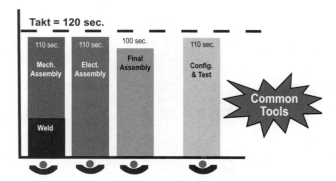

Operator Balance Chart—Part B
(Sensor-Activated Arm)

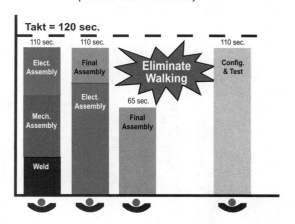

Operator Balance Chart—Part C
(Manually Activated Arm)

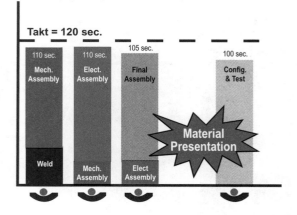

Current State

Future State

Operator Balance Chart—Part D
(Barcode Diverter Piston)

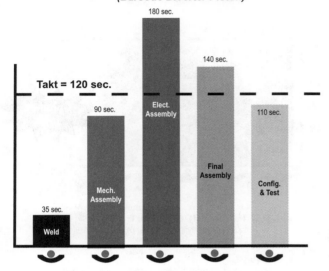

Operator Balance Chart—Part D
(Barcode Diverter Piston)

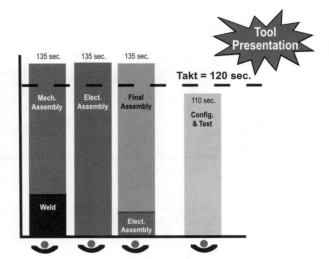

Tool Presentation

Operator Balance Chart—Part E
(Barcode Diverter Arm)

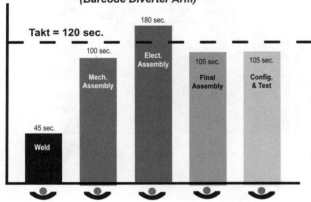

Operator Balance Chart—Part E
(Barcode Diverter Arm)

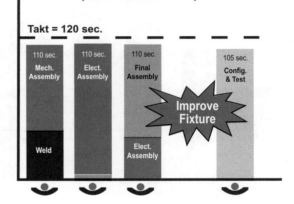

Improve Fixture

Operator Balance Chart—Part F
(Sensor-Activated Piston)

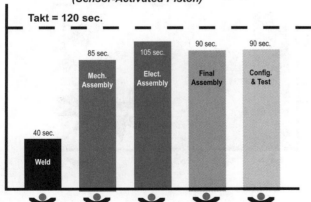

Operator Balance Chart—Part F
(Sensor-Activated Piston)

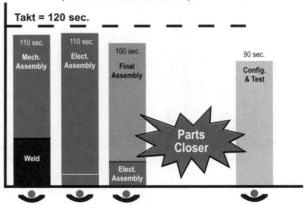

Parts Closer

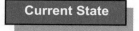

Current State

Operator Balance Chart—Part G
(Laser-Activiated Piston)

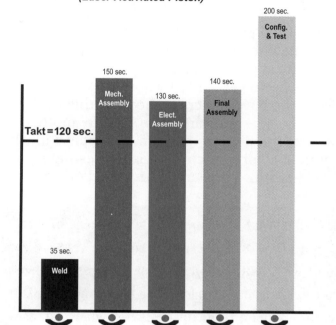

Future State

Operator Balance Chart—Part G
(Laser-Activiated Piston)

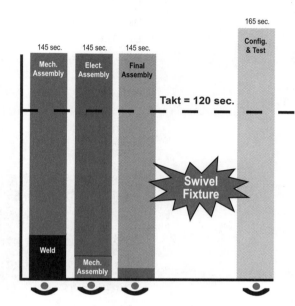

Operator Balance Chart—Part H
(Manually Activated Piston)

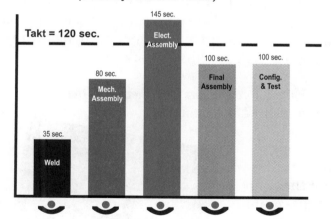

Operator Balance Chart—Part H
(Manually Activated Piston)

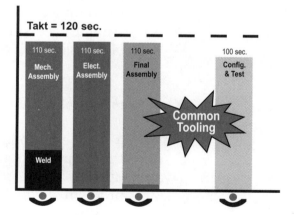

These balance charts reveal a problem. Product D and product G exceed takt time and cannot be balanced to our planned cycle time of 110 seconds. Product G also has a test cycle that exceeds our planned cycle time by 90 seconds. We discussed this with the management team at EMC and decided that while it was feasible to reduce the work content of the products, it couldn't be done quickly. Time-consuming new tooling and product changes would be needed. We indicate this on our future-state value stream map with a kaizen event; however, to get started before these changes are made, we must decide how we can create flow for this family, as two products exceed takt time and cannot be built in another product family. We will have to discuss more on this topic with the team to identify our options. Our first concern is the testing equipment, as this has a fixed machine cycle and a dedicated operator.

In the future state, we will target a maximum work content of 440 seconds (110 seconds cycle time × 4 operators) knowing that we can reduce the work content with tooling and product changes. However, we will show this as an event that will take place over a period of time. We could also create a "long term future state" where we consider long-term changes and illustrate them.

The balance charts also show that we only need four operators (verses the current five operators used) on six of the products to still make takt time. What should we do with the operators that are not needed in our future state? If we lay them off, what kind of message will that send to the remaining operators?

Remember, when we make improvements and then layoff employees, that is the last improvement we will be making!

One method for making these operators valuable to the operation is to educate them in problem solving and continuous improvement, then place them into a cell with the statement, "Your job is to eliminate your job," meaning the goal is to eliminate enough waste that the person will no longer be needed in the cell. In this method every one in the cell

Management can show their commitment to lean by stating there will not be any layoffs due to lean improvements. When waste is removed and less people are needed, this should be done naturally through attrition.

knows who is leaving when the waste is eliminated. After the worker's job in the cell has been eliminated, he or she moves on to the next cell and performs this process again. This method makes employees active agents in implementing lean, not targets for cost-cutting measures.

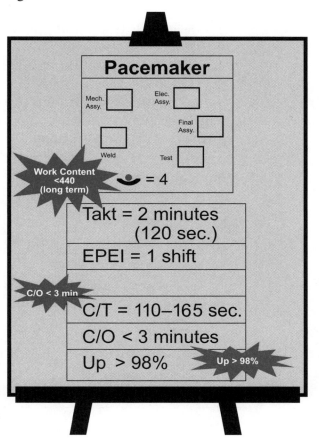

BALANCING MACHINE CYCLES

There may be operations for some products that we cannot balance to takt time due to machine cycle times, such as the testing station for product G. Our first approach is to examine the machine itself for waste. Can we use auto-eject? Can we move parts closer? Can the cycle be reduced? These questions and more should be asked and answered in order to reduce waste and improve balance. If we cannot balance the machine after the waste has been eliminated, we should look at the mix of the product family and determine if the products with the longer cycle times will cause us to exceed our planned interval. For this we use an *average weighted cycle time* (AWCT). An average weighted cycle time considers the volume of each product in the mix along with its respective cycle time. This helps to determine the impact that products whose cycle time exceed takt time will have on the overall mix performance.

Mathematically, it is equal to:

Sum (Cycle time × Part demand)/Total demand

The testing station at EMC has a fixed machine cycle. Product G exceeds the takt time by 90 seconds, while other products beat the takt time. Even though product G exceeds the takt time, we may be able to gain back this time with other products. To find out if this is true, we will calculate the AWCT for the testing station.

Testing Equipment

Product Code	Product Name	Cycle Time (C/T)	Demand (per day)	C/T x Demand
A	Sensor-Activated Arm	110 sec	65	7150 sec
B	Laser-Activated Arm	110 sec	85	9350 sec
C	Manually Activated Arm	100 sec	35	3500 sec
D	Barcode Diverter Piston	110 sec	70	7700 sec
E	Barcode Diverter Arm	105 sec	50	5250 sec
F	Sensor-Activated Piston	90 sec	55	4950 sec
G	Laser-Activated Piston	200 sec	20	4000 sec
H	Manually Activated Piston	100 sec	25	2500 sec
X	Custom Orders	110 sec	45	4950 sec
		Sum (C/T x Demand) =		**49,350 seconds**
	Total Demand = 450 units			

Average weighted cycle time = 49,350 sec./450 units = 110 sec.

This means we can handle about 20 of product G in our mix each day and just meet our planned cycle time of 110 seconds. Any more volume of product G will not allow us to build the total volume of 450 units per day. To illustrate the machine balance, we created a machine cycle balance chart. This is similar to the operator balance chart, except we will use machine cycles and show the AWCT compared to takt and planned cycle time (PCT).

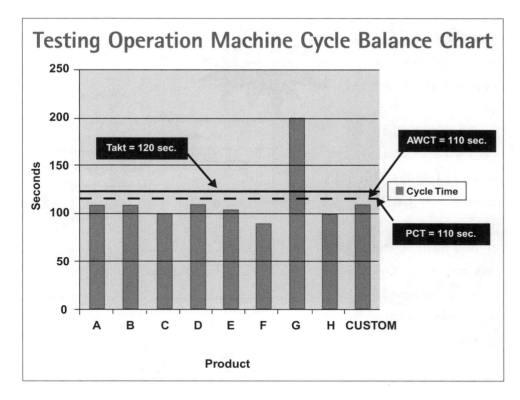

IDENTIFYING THE TRUE PACEMAKER

Since the machine cycle of product G exceeds takt time, we will not be able to have continuous flow from assembly through testing. We will need to gain back the time lost while processing product G. Therefore, we must always have units available when the short cycle test units are completed prior to takt time. *We will need some inventory between the pacemaker and testing.* For this we will need a FIFO lane between assembly and testing. Since inventory will stop and accumulate between assembly and testing, these are now *two different processes*. However, they are located physically in the same area, only steps away. We will represent this on our future-state map by connecting the process boxes with a dotted line.

When we selected our pacemaker, we assumed the tester would be included (since it could be dedicated to this product family). This is no longer true! The pacemaker should have continuous one-piece flow with no stoppages or accumulation of inventory.

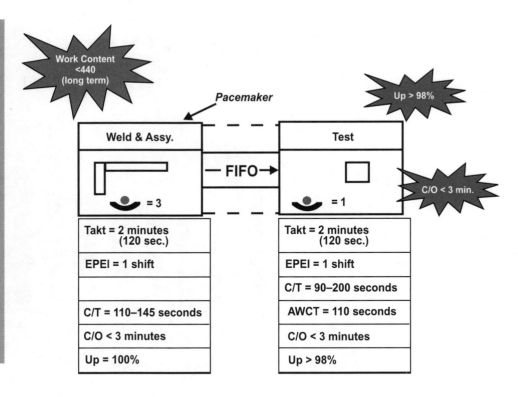

Sizing the FIFO Lane

We know that for each product G we build in succession, products will back up at the tester and more space in the FIFO lane will be needed. To estimate the size of the FIFO lane, we determine the imbalance of the pacemaker process versus the testing process and multiply these by the volume required, then divide by takt time.

For example: Product G takes 200 seconds to test, while the takt time is 120 seconds. Therefore, 200 – 120 = 80 seconds. This means for every product G we build in succession, we have to buffer or hold 80 seconds worth of work in front of testing. Our AWCT calculated that we could handle a volume of 20 pieces of product G. Therefore:

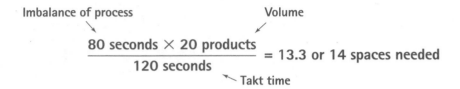

For now, we will start with a FIFO lane that can hold 15 units in order to allow for changes in demand. We can also continuously

> We must make sure that when the FIFO lane gets filled, the pacemaker will stop. Otherwise inventory and lead times will increase. This is an important step in changing culture.

improve the testing time of product G to reduce the size of the FIFO lane.

In this calculation we stated: "For each product G we build in succession. What if we do not build all 20 together?" If we can "sprinkle in" the product G throughout the day, then a much smaller FIFO lane is needed. In order to accomplish this, we need to further reduce changeover times and allow for more changeovers per shift. This allows us to produce smaller amounts of product G at one time, greatly reducing the inventory between the processes. *This is yet another reason why smaller intervals are better*.

MATERIAL PRESENTATION

We can also tell from the balance charts that each station needs to be flexible to run a mix of products. Also, the materials needed for each product must be presented at the right time to the operator. This can be challenging with a high variety of products. Therefore, we must develop a strategy for component parts—A Plan for Every Part.

A plan for every part means that we will develop a plan for each component part in the product family. This plan will outline information such as:

- What size bin the part is kept in.
- How many parts are kept in the bin (this may be an estimate).
- How the parts will be replenished: for example small parts such as screws, nuts, and bolts may be replenished by the operator from a supply at the station, while other parts may be replenished by the material handler who follows at a preset interval and sets routes for component delivery (these are sometimes called water spider routes).
- How often the bin will be replenished.
- Where the supply of parts are kept (warehouse location or line storage).
- The name of the cell where the part is used for the specific product.
- Any special requirements (e.g. roller conveyor feeding box to operator).

We may also have to be creative in presenting the variety of material to the operator. Devices such as turntables that are divided into sections and hold a supply of parts (and perhaps tooling) for different products in each section may be useful. As a different product is needed, the operator rotates the turntable to the corresponding section. Rollaway carts that hold component parts for products are another way to present material in a high-mix environment. As different products are needed, the operator rolls away the current cart and rolls in the new one. The material handler replenishes all parts on the roll away carts without interrupting the operator.

Material presentation for a high mix of products will take some creativity and planning. This is an area where we will have to sweat the details.

The Pacemaker Loop

Weld & Assy.	Max. 15	Test
= 3	— FIFO →	= 1

Pacemaker

C/O < 3 min.

Up > 98%

Takt = 2 minutes (120 sec.)	Takt = 2 minutes (120 sec.)
EPEI = 1 shift	EPEI = 1 shift
	C/T = 90–200 seconds
C/T 110–145 seconds	AWCT = 110 seconds
C/O < 3 minutes	C/O < 3 minutes
Up = 100%	Up > 98%

Work Content <440 (long term)

SUMMARY

When creating balance charts we need to break down the work into individual work elements. We should not add elements that are strictly waste, and easily removable, into the balance charts. Once we have the elements needed, we can balance work to the planned cycle time. We target a planned cycle time of 92 to 95 percent of takt time to allow for variation. Balance charts are done for labor (in a machine environment, they can also be done for machine cycles). When machine cycles are fixed and cannot be easily changed, we can use a small FIFO lane to separate the processes and balance the different cycle times.

What Have We Done So Far with the EMC Team?

At this point we have taught the EMC Management team how to:

- ❏ Create operator balance charts for the product family
- ❏ Determine the planned cycle time needed
- ❏ Create a continuous one-piece flow pacemaker cell
- ❏ Use FIFO lanes where machine cycle times exceed takt time
- ❏ Use average weighted cycle times for machines cycles that exceed takt

The team likes this strategy and understands it will require some cross-training of the operators to be successful. The benefits will be realized in the flexibility to respond to changing customer demand.

What's Next for the Team?

Our next step is to work with the team to determine how to create flow for the pacemaker, as some products' (D and G) balance charts show that they exceed takt time. There is no other area to make these in, so we must develop a strategy for flow that includes them. We will teach the team:

- ❏ Four basic options for balancing for flow for products with varying work content
- ❏ Workstation layout to support flow
- ❏ How to handle changeovers at the pacemaker

QUESTION 6—
How Will We Balance Flow for the Mix?

I f all products in the Arms & Pistons family contained similar work content with only a small variation, they might flow through the pacemaker with some variation, but at the end of the interval we should be able to produce the products required. Some variation would occur at the last station, as we have balanced the other stations to our planned cycle time and left this station to fluctuate based on work content. Some products take longer to produce than the takt time given. This causes the pacemaker to slow down when they run. This may happen even if products are within 30 percent work content of each other. *Remember, 30 percent is just a guideline to select product families. You may change the product families after reviewing the balance charts.*

BALANCING PRODUCTS WITH HIGH WORK CONTENT INTO THE FAMILY

If a product has a work content greater than 30 percent due to labor and must still be built within the product family (such as our product G), there are a few choices we can make. We can either limit the amount of this product we will make per interval

We could also increase the interval, but as we mentioned before, this is not a good option as it decreases flexibility.

(as these products will otherwise disrupt takt time), store more finished goods, work overtime, or utilize extra operators and stations when these products are made. In other words, we can either keep labor constant at the pacemaker and level the schedule, or *we can balance each product to the planned cycle time and vary the labor to try and build to demand.* There are several ways to approach each of these choices.

The following options can be used when a product's work content causes it to exceed the takt time with a constant number of operators. These are not the only options; we are just presenting a few to get us moving in the right direction. Which option we use will depend highly upon the type of company we are in terms of demand variation, volume, and type of products produced.

Most of these options involve the use of a *finished-goods supermarket,* a controlled inventory of items that is used to schedule production at an upstream process through visual control or kanban (a signaling system usually using cards). When inventory in the supermarket is depleted to a predefined level, a signal is sent to the supplying process to replace the depleted inventory up to a predefined maximum level. For more information on supermarkets, refer to *Learning to See* listed in the "Important Sources" on p. 189.

Balancing Options

To make a simple example, let's pretend our product family contains three products with varying work content. Products A, B, and C have a labor work content of 90, 110, and 150 seconds, respectively. Product C is outside of the 30 percent work content guideline. Customer demand is steady at 450 products per day, 150 of each product. This creates a takt time of two minutes (120 seconds) over two shifts. How could we balance these products?

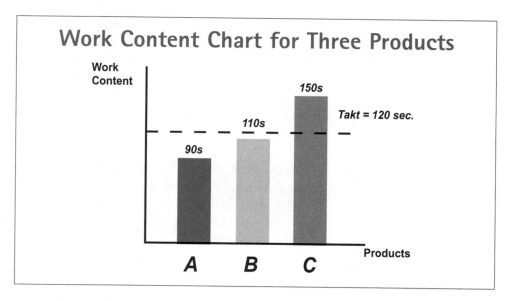

Option 1: Level the schedule and keep labor constant—build products in fixed sequence.

If we built the products in order of A, C, B we would always yield three products in just under 6 minutes. Every hour, 30 products would be produced, 10 of each item. We would level the production at the pacemaker by providing a sequence of orders based on work content. In other words, we would arrange the orders coming out of the supermarket to build high work content products only after low work products. When a high-content product hits the pacemaker, the pacemaker would slow down and not produce the product at the same output as other products. In this method we create an "average takt time" to flow to along with a consistent pitch increment (we will talk more about pitch on pp. 117–134).

Option #1:

- **Discrete Parts**
- **Low Demand Variation**
- **High Volume**

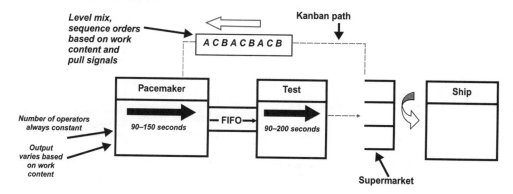

This option works well when demand is steady and we can afford to level the schedule at least a few weeks out. Very little waste is incurred at the pacemaker. Output varies at the pacemaker when the high-content products hit. We do have inventory, but we get a nice, consistent flow in the value stream, allowing constant withdrawal of work at preset times from the pacemaker.

However, what would happen if demand changed daily? What if the next day the customer wanted 450 products, 90 A's, 150 B's, and 210 C's? In this case we would have to work overtime or carry a high variety and significant amount of finished goods to level the schedule, and we would incur the waste of inventory and overproduction.

Option 2: Level the schedule and build ahead. Keep labor constant, use FIFO to shipping.

In this option we keep labor constant and build ahead of the demand. We build to a FIFO lane to the shipping department. Production control reviews customer orders a few days ahead of lead time and sequence them based on work content. The daily production of the pacemaker varies, as the products with higher work content take longer to produce. The pacemaker "pulses" at different speeds, depending upon the mix, while the FIFO lane absorbs this pulse.

Option #2:
- Discrete Parts
- Custom Parts
- Low Demand Variation

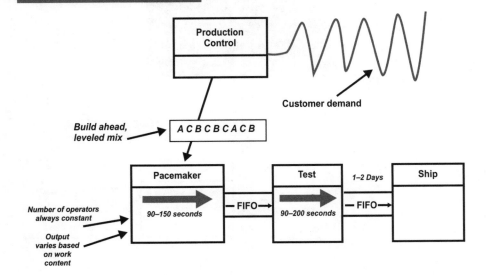

This is often a good option, as it levels the schedule and contains less waste than a supermarket. The inventory is already sold, so it doesn't sit there long. This option works well when the pacemaker process is at the end of the value stream, close to the customer, and we can afford to level the schedule at least a few days ahead of lead time. It also allows us to build custom products in the same value stream with the same lead time as normal items.

This option may be difficult if the pacemaker is upstream, as the product must flow in FIFO through remaining processes to get to shipping. If the processes downstream of the pacemaker pulse differently than the pacemaker (as different products may take longer at these processes), the FIFO lanes may tend to become larger to absorb the variations at each process. This may increase lead time and force us to know what customers want more than a few days ahead of lead time with firm orders.

What if there is a high demand variation? What if the customer orders a high amount of product C with a high work content? Let's look at another option.

Option 3: Level the schedule with a supermarket and build to ship with FIFO.

In this option we place commodity items (those that are steady sellers) in a finished-goods supermarket. We use this as an overflow buffer or safety stock. Labor remains constant and production control levels the orders based on work content. When we can't meet the demand for today due to the variety of orders and work content needed, we pull from the commodity items stored in the supermarket and build what we can to customer order. On days when demand is down we build to replenish the supermarket store.

This option works well when handling a large variety of products. It provides a level schedule at the pacemaker, which allows us to use the same number of operators each day. By placing only commodity items in the supermarket, we decrease the needed inventory.

In this option, we still need to know what the customer wants at least a few days ahead of lead time in order to provide the leveled schedule, and the pacemaker still pulses at different speeds. We will not have consistent daily output from the pacemaker. If

Option #3:
- **Discrete Parts**
- **Custom Parts**
- **High Demand Variation**

our tester also runs at different speeds, this could make for lengthy FIFO lanes. Is there a way to respond more quickly when the customer wants his order tomorrow?

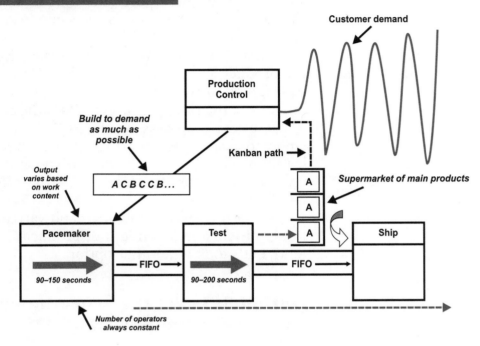

Option 4: Balance to takt time and add labor when a product exceeds takt time. Try to build products to demand.

Another option is to balance each product to a planned cycle time of 110 seconds and add labor when a product exceeds takt time. In this case, we may need another operator to help when product C is built.

This option is useful if there are processes between the pacemaker and shipping, or when the assembly of custom products is in the same value stream as discrete products (as custom products can be delivered in the same time as discrete products). It provides consistent speed through the value stream, as the output of the pacemaker is constant. It is also a good option when we don't know what customers will order tomorrow, and we don't want to build the wrong products and carry inventory. The lead time is shorter and we are carrying less inventory, which consists of only steady selling items. Of course, there is a trade-off. We must add and remove operators based on the product mix, and build products in a small batch based on labor content—which may prove difficult.

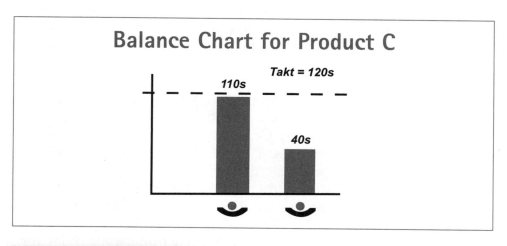

Option #4:
• Discrete Parts
• Custom Parts
• High Demand Variation
• Short Lead Times

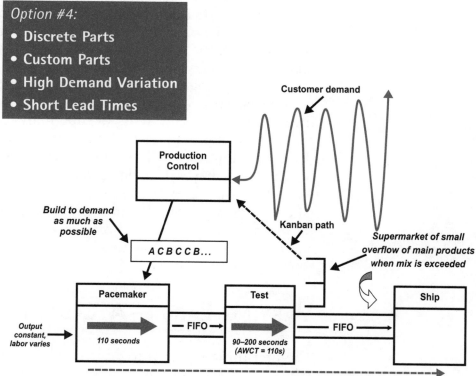

Choosing an Option

To recap, our four options are:

- ❑ Use a finished goods supermarket and level the schedule.
- ❑ Level the schedule and build ahead in FIFO to shipping.
- ❑ Use a combination of supermarket and FIFO to keep labor constant.
- ❑ Balance each product to the mix takt time and vary labor to try and build to demand, with a small supermarket to help us with variation in demand.

To decide which way to go we look at our business in terms of mix and demand (this was illustrated earlier in "Welcome to EMC Supply Company" under "What Kind of Manufacturer Is EMC?," pp. 19–20). EMC Supply determined that they were a discrete manufacturer with a high variation of demand. They cannot use a finished-goods supermarket for every product to level the schedule, as this would require significant inventory. Building ahead is difficult, as they supply parts for repair when the customer's equipment is down; the customer calls today for shipment tomorrow. When customers do order ahead, they constantly change their orders at the last minute. For EMC Supply it seems the best option (the one with the least amount of waste) is to balance the mix to takt time and vary the labor to try and build to demand. We know they won't be able to build to demand each day, due to customer volume variation. Therefore, they will carry a small finished-goods inventory of the main items (a supermarket). This will act as a buffer, allowing them to pull product when demand is high. When demand is low, they will produce parts to refill the supermarket. So, in effect, they will build to demand as much as possible and when they can't they'll do some leveling of the schedule using finished goods. Adding operators when needed to balance the pacemaker is not easy to do and may seem inefficient from the factory standpoint. Therefore, we need to take a closer look at this option to really investigate it.

VARYING LABOR—A CLOSER LOOK

The first thing we need to do is review our operator balance charts. We revise these to balance all products at the pacemaker to the planned cycle time of 110 seconds by adding additional operators. Let's go back to products D and products G, as these exceeded the takt time, and rebalance them to the planned cycle time of 110 seconds (see pp. 81–83 for the earlier balance charts).

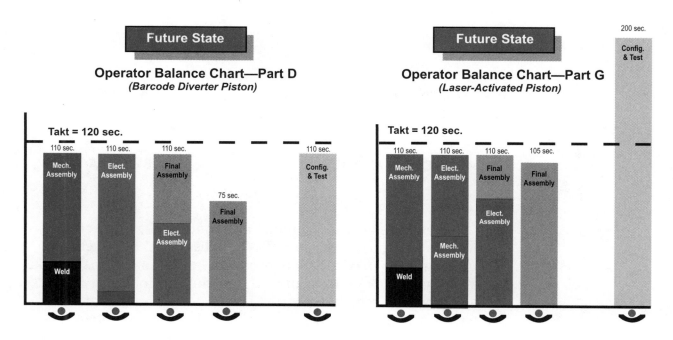

It will take four operators at the pacemaker to obtain the planned cycle time of 110 seconds with these products. After reviewing all the products, we have summarized our findings as follows:

3 OPERATORS		4 OPERATORS	
Product Code	Product Name	Product Code	Product Name
A	Sensor-Activated Arm	D	Barcode Diverter Piston
B	Laser-Activated Arm	G	Laser-Activated Piston
C	Manually Activated Arm		
E	Barcode Diverter Arm		
F	Sensor-Activated Piston		
H	Manually Activated Piston		

Moving people in and out of a cell when certain products run can cause difficulties in personnel management and scheduling. We must also decide where the operator will go when he or she leaves the cell. In the ideal situation we would have an operator move between two or three cells to perform the work needed on the high-cycle products. However, in reality we would schedule the products that require more labor together to minimize having operators jumping in the middle of the work shift to different cells. Take our previous example (p. 95); it may be easiest to run product C at the beginning of the shift, then send it to another product family whose high-content products run toward the end of the shift.

Operator added at the beginning of the shift

Operator leaves and works in another cell

C C C C C C C C C . . . . . A B A B B B A B A

(Mix changes daily)

As mentioned earlier, running all products G for the shift together is going to cause the FIFO lane between the pacemaker and testing to be maximum (as product G exceeds pacemaker takt time and will stack up in front of the testing station), but it will make it easier to schedule people. This is a trade-off situation as we strive to reduce the cycle time of product G. Remember, this product was outside of the product family guidelines but we were forced to fit it in. As a compromise, it may be a good idea to alternate products G and D at the pacemaker, as this will reduce the number of product G that run in succession and reduce the size of the FIFO lane. Both products require four operators, but only product G is over takt time at the tester.

Workstation Layout

When we vary labor to build to demand, we need enough workstations to balance the product with the highest work content and still make takt time. Therefore, we may have empty stations when other products are produced. Having empty workstations in the cell is okay, just try to have them at the end of the cell so they don't increase the walking needed by operators.

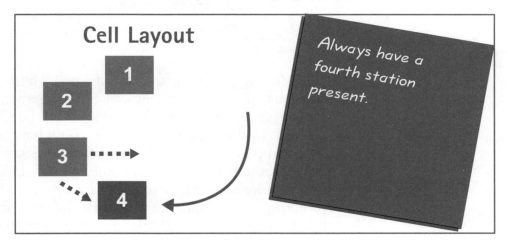

Cell Layout

1
2
3
4

Always have a fourth station present.

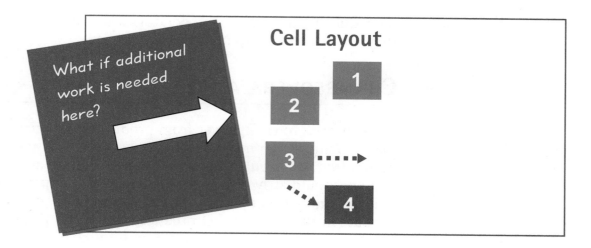

Dance Steps

Sometimes, additional work will be needed in the middle of the cell and cannot be avoided. In this case we need to "alter the dance steps." Dance steps refer to the way people flow through a cell. We can create different paths through the cell, depending upon the staffing of that cell. Each staffing level of the cell should have its steps clearly identified, so all operators know their pre-scribed movements through the cell. This will reduce as much waste as possible.

For more information on people flow cell design, refer to *Creating Continuous Flow* listed in "Important Sources" section on p. 189.

When we vary the labor and use additional stations, we should also balance the stations at the beginning of the cell to have the same amount of work in each, leaving variations for the stations at the end of the cell. This approach allows us to continuously improve the process, to reduce the overall work content, and to eliminate the partial station at the end. It also allows the operator to access the workstation without disrupting the cell and to move to other cells easily.

As we mentioned earlier, in using this method we will always have an empty station in place—but what about the operator? If the operator cannot work in another cell, this may be a good time for him or her to work on standard work sheets (covered in "Visual Method Sheets," pp. 111–112), 5'S (workplace organization: sort, set in order, shine, standardize, sustain), problem solving, visual systems, changeover reduction, or replenishing bins for other operators. We must make sure that the operator does not work ahead and overproduce. One good way to ensure this is to provide a list of ongoing continuous improvement projects (from the value stream maps), so operators know what to work on if they are not needed to build products.

CHANGEOVERS AT THE PACEMAKER

We still need to changeover from product to product at the pacemaker. With a high mix of product, we know this may happen quite often. We would like zero changeover time at the pacemaker, and we should strive to make this happen. The use of universal fixtures, and permanently mounted color-coded tools for each product in the mix, can help reduce changeover time. In reality, we still may need to allow a little time for changeovers.

Knowing that our goal is a changeover time of zero, we kaizen the changeover times to reduce them as much as possible. Each assembly process at EMC Supply currently has a changeover time of one to two minutes. With work, the team feels it could get that down to 30 seconds or less, as the stations are generic. EMC Supply has developed a future state with an EPEI of one shift. This means they will do at least nine changeovers (eight standard products + one custom product) per shift. We could go back and reduce our planned cycle time by a few seconds and redo the operator balance charts to cover this. However, we allowed for a planned cycle time that is 8 percent faster than takt time, and this may be enough. For now, we will add one minute to each pitch increment (we will talk more about pitch increments on pp. 117–134) and monitor the progress. If we consistently fall short and must pull finished goods to meet the customer demand, we may go back and adjust the planned cycle time later to account for this.

If the total time needed for changeovers is high and we cannot kaizen this down without significant capital investment, one option is to allow for this in the planned cycle time. The other options are the same as when a machine cannot support the interval (see the previous section, p. 70).

Finalizing the Balance

We have now reviewed and decided upon our balancing technique for the pacemaker. We updated our whiteboard to illustrate what we decided. We added production control and a schedule box to our future-state design to illustrate that production control will be leveling orders between the supermarket and customers. We will discuss the leveling technique in detail in the upcoming sections.

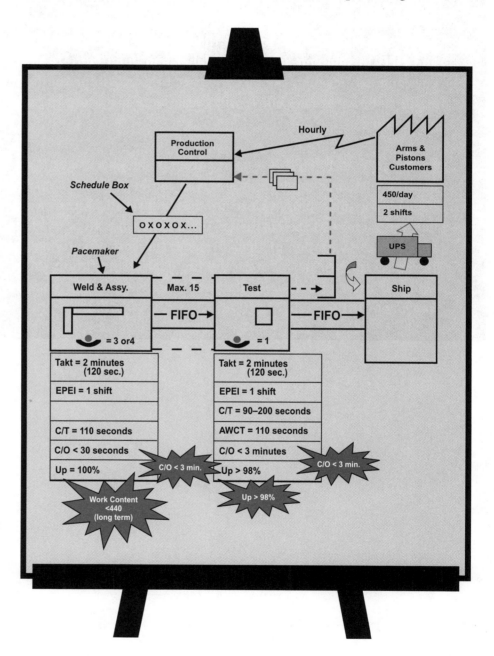

SUMMARY

When we balance for a mix of products to run through the pacemaker, we strive to balance all products to run at the same cycle time through the pacemaker. When this is not possible due to varying work content, we balance as many stations as possible to takt time, leaving the imbalance at the end. When work content varies enough to require more operators than others on some products, we have to decide whether to level the schedule with a supermarket, build ahead and FIFO to shipping, or vary the labor and build more to demand. In a high-mix environment, leveling the mix is easier to execute for the factory, as it is more stable and repeatable, but it will cause more inventory to be built than is needed at the time.

Building ahead to FIFO is a good option if the pacemaker is close to the customer and the customer can lock in orders ahead of lead time. Varying labor is more difficult for the factory to execute but will result in less inventory and will closely link the factory to the customer. The decision has to be made by each company based on the variation of their demand, the cost of carrying their inventory, the flexibility of their labor force, and the goal of the future state. We should look at which of these options will eliminate more waste in the company and strive to implement it.

What Have We Done So Far with the EMC Team?

Now we have taught the management team at EMC some of the techniques to balance the mix of products through their pacemaker.

These include:

❐ Leveling the schedule and maintaining constant labor
❐ Leveling the schedule and building ahead to orders
❐ Leveling the schedule using a supermarket with constant labor
❐ Balancing to takt by varying labor and building more to demand, using a supermarket as an overflow

At EMC we decided to balance to takt and vary labor in order to closely build to customer demand. We discussed briefly the concept of moving people between cells. The EMC team stated that they move people to different areas now, depending upon what products are falling behind. This usually happens when they are "firefighting" to get production out. Moving people will not be an issue for EMC. In fact, they began to see that the methods outlined would work for their products and would extinguish fires before they began!

What's Next for the Team?

Our next step is to work with the team to make the pacemaker perform consistently, no matter what product is run. Therefore we need to teach the team:

❐ That consistent performance is needed to counter the variability of customer demand
❐ That standard work creates consistency
❐ How to find the best method
❐ How to implement method changes
❐ How to document standard work

QUESTION 7—
How Will We Create Standard Work for the Mix?

After discussing in detail the concepts of flow in a mixed model environment, the management team at EMC Supply began to understand how they could apply these concepts to their products. However, they soon began to realize that a high variety of products in the same cell would require the operators to learn and remember how to build each product correctly. They would also have to perform the work in the same amount of time each time. Otherwise, how would they ever hope to consistently balance the cycle time to the takt time? The team was concerned that setting up a cell in this manner would lead to quality problems along with poor productivity. We shared this concern and explained that there is a key element needed to create flow in a high-mix environment. That element is *standard work*.

By standard work we mean that *any operator following a prescribed method, with a proper workstation and proper tools, should be able to perform the amount of work required in the same amount of time, with perfect quality, without risk to health or safety*. This means that any operator should be able to work on any product in the cell, or at any workstation in the cell, and perform the work needed in the time needed. It also means that if we were to take a random snapshot of the amount of work-in-process in a cell, it would always be the same amount at any time. This sounds like quite a challenging task, but it is not as hard to achieve as it seems.

Different operators often perform the same tasks differently. Therefore, each operator will complete the task in different times. *The key to creating standard work is developing consistent methods from operator balance charts*. If each operator can follow the same method, the time to perform the work will become more consistent. Our goal is to drive out variability. Without a documented method to perform the work, the cycle time of the stations will vary widely, causing work stoppages in the cell, overproduction, and/or our customers not getting their orders on time.

Finding the current best method (remember—the best method is the one with the least amount of waste) or a method that everyone can agree upon, seems like a difficult task. Engineers can prescribe methods, but operators may not want to follow them. So how do we develop and establish methods? We do so by openly stating that this is a starting point, and that operators and engineers together should continuously improve these methods. Engineers possess the knowledge of ergonomics: balance charting, safety, tooling, efficiency, and product knowledge; while operators possess the hands-on product knowledge that comes with having built products for many years. It sounds like a good fit to eliminate waste, *and it is!*

To provide the current best method, engineers and operators must work together with a common goal of eliminating waste. They must also work to continuously reduce waste. For example, an engineer might prescribe a method to the operators. After a few days of running, the operators might realize that a certain station is falling behind and cannot always make takt, (hopefully the engineer was around to observe this fact). During the day, the operators might wish to stop and review the methods used at that station with their team members, the value stream manager, and the engineer. If an operator has an idea on a new method, then scientific method is used to validate the new method: hypothesize, test, analyze, implement, and extend. The engineer

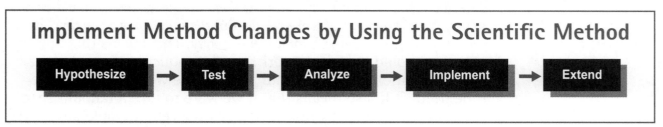

Implement Method Changes by Using the Scientific Method

Hypothesize → Test → Analyze → Implement → Extend

should check ergonomics, safety, and tooling issues. If the method removes waste and allows the station to perform better, and fits with the value stream plan, the new method should be adopted and documented.

DOCUMENTING STANDARD WORK

In a repetitive environment where few products are built and takt times are small (let's say under one minute or so), the standard work may be relatively easy to document and post where everyone can see it at a glance. This may include the key work elements to be performed and their associated times, a standard work chart of the sequence, and safety and quality checks. Sometimes, where a total productive maintenance (TPM) program is used by the organization, it includes preventative maintenance steps. It may even have examples or photos of poor-quality items. Statistical process control (SPC) may be in use to predict tool failure and bad quality.

However, in a high-mix environment, takt time may be higher (for lower-volume, high-content products), along with a high variety of products. So creating standard work for longer takt times (e.g., four hours of work) on a wide variety of products is not an easy task, but it must be done to combat variability! Remember that we want to give ourselves a reasonable "management time-frame" to spot production problems. (We will talk about this on pp. 117–119.)

VISUAL METHOD SHEETS

To assist the operators in following a consistent method for each product at each station, visual method sheets may be used. *The key to visual method sheets is to make them visual.* Method sheets with paragraphs of text on them are not effective. Operators do not take the time to read them until they are having difficulty or have produced bad product. Pictures, icons, and symbols can convey operator work and critical areas. Operators can reference these at a glance *prior* to building a product. Visual method sheets provide a quick reference for operators and remind them how this product is built at this station. The difficult part of using visual method sheets is remembering to update them when methods have been improved. One way to do this is to follow the scientific method, mentioned previously, to implement a new idea. Once an idea has been approved and the method is changed, allow the operators to change the visual method sheets. This provides ownership to the operators for the sheets and helps make sure they are always correct and up to date. Correct visual method sheets might also be added as a cell performance measurement (examples of visual method sheets can be found on the accompanying CD).

Mounting the Method Sheets

With a large number of products running through the cell, the number of method sheets can grow quickly. Presenting all the method sheets needed at a station can require some thought. One method for presenting a large number of sheets is to use a large Rolodex type holder. The sheets could be arranged by product, at each station, in these holders—perhaps using color-coding for quick identification. As a different product entered the station, the operator could simply reference the file for the correct set of method sheets by flipping the Rolodex to the correct standard work sheet.

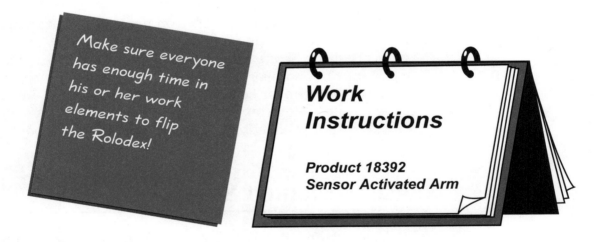

Make sure everyone has enough time in his or her work elements to flip the Rolodex!

Work Instructions

Product 18392
Sensor Activated Arm

Another method for presenting multiple sheets is to use computer monitors at stations. In this method the operator performs a small step of work (maybe a minute or so), then presses "enter" to see the next sheet. This works well when takt times are very large (two hours or greater), or when there is a concern as to whether the correct engineering revision of a blueprint or method sheet will be viewed. Also, take care when mounting the standard work sheets. These should be at eye level, out of the work path, and not interfering with product flow.

SMART TOOLS AND STANDARD WORK

One of the latest areas of development in standard work and quality is the use of smart tools. *Smart tools refers to integrating tools used at a station with the visual method sheet used at that station.* This requires the use of a computer monitor at the station and sensors on each of the tools. For example, if a method sheet prescribed that a nut is torque to 20 in-lbs., and the electric ratchet only applied 17 in-lbs., the computer would not let the operator advance the screen to perform the next steps. An error light would be indicated on the screen to show that the correct method was not followed and a quality problem may exist. This method can also ensure that each component has been picked from bins prior to passing work to the next station. This technology will take *poka-yoke* (mistake-proofing) to the next level.

> It's good standard work if it's written in a language that you don't speak and you can still understand it!!!

LONG TAKT TIME

It should be noted that some companies produce products that may require a takt time of hours. These are usually complex products with relatively low demand (three to four per month). In this case, care must be used to develop standard work.

Several tools can be used to help reduce the variation in high cycle time:

- A computer monitor for a high number of visual method sheets at one station

- Work broken into sections, each with its own standard work

- White boards that indicate standard work times with reference to assembly manuals

- Poka-yoke (mistake-proofing)

- Timing indicators that let operators know where they are on the visual method sheet verses takt time

SUMMARY

Standard work may take time and effort to implement and maintain. However, developing and implementing standard work also changes culture. Like other techniques in lean manufacturing, it allows waste to been seen and provides operators with the opportunity to problem-solve and continuously improve. As we mentioned previously, you might have to "sweat the details" in a complex environment to implement a future state that will greatly reduce waste and build a culture that will continuously improve.

What Have We Done So Far with the EMC Team?

As a quick review, the team at EMC has worked with us to create a pacemaker for their future state. The properties of the pacemaker include:

- ❑ The ability to provide any product in the product family of Arms & Pistons at a takt time of two minutes consistently
- ❑ Continuous one-piece flow, from welding to final assembly
- ❑ Standard work developed so that no matter what product in the family runs through the cell, the operators have standard methods and can perform the work consistently

Although they saw quite a bit of work ahead of them, the team became very excited. They understood the concepts of the mixed model cell and what they had to do. There were still questions to answer and details to decide, but the team knew that they would resolve them as they began to implement their future state and continuously improve it.

What's Next for the Team?

We will need to discuss how we can create a management time frame at the pacemaker so we know how the pacemaker is performing. This will include:

- ❑ Defining pitch
- ❑ Creating pitch at the pacemaker
- ❑ Developing the schedule box

PART IV:
PITCH AND SCHEDULING

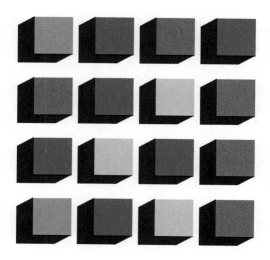

QUESTION 8—
How Will We Create the Pitch at the Pacemaker?

Pitch *refers to how often we release and take away work from the pacemaker. It provides us with a management time frame.*[1] It is a measurement of how the value stream, or more specifically the pacemaker, is performing to our schedule. If we set a schedule for a week, it will take us a week before we know we have met the schedule. If we set a schedule for a day, it will take us a day before we know we have met the schedule. What if we schedule every hour? The pitch increment should be small enough to allow us to react to problems and still ship to customers on time.

- Takt = the customer demand rate
- Planned cycle time = the rate we produce at to meet customer demand
- Pitch = how we measure the pacemaker to see if it is attaining takt

---

1. *Learning to See*. Mike Rother and John Shook. The Lean Enterprise Institute, 1999, pp. 51–52.

Pitch sets the value stream in motion, then measures its performance. Establishing a consistent increment of work that is released and removed from the pacemaker at specified time intervals can do this. It is always helpful if these time intervals are multiples of the takt time. By having a regulated pace that removes work from the pacemaker, we can see if the pacemaker is underproducing or overproducing several times during the shift. This allows everyone to see if the pacemaker flow is in line with takt time. We use this method to physically synchronize the factory and spot problems very quickly without waiting for the end of the day's production run. Preset material-handling loops, performed at preset times, provide rhythm throughout the day. Using pitch, it is easy to spot when a process is out of rhythm and not producing to takt.

The concept of pitch can be explained by thinking of a train station inside the factory. Trains run at preset times along specific routes that do not change. People must get on the train at specific times, or they miss it and have to wait until the next train comes along. We can use the same concept to create pitch in the factory. Our material handlers (like trains) will run at preset times. Products (like people at real train stations) must get on the train at a certain time or they will miss it. If products miss the train, we know something is wrong and we must enter into a problem-solving mode. This method is very visual and drives home the need for discipline and standard work, which are key elements in lean.

In the factory we can implement pitch by creating routes for the material handlers to follow. The material handlers would run the regular routes at pre-set intervals. A typical route would be for the material handler to start at the shipping deck (where he had just dropped off the last part), then go to the schedule box and pick up a schedule, bring the schedule to the cell, pick up what the cell made (from the last schedule that was dropped off), and bring that to the shipping deck. Material handlers may pick up multiple schedules and stop at multiple cells before returning to the shipping deck.

Standard Routes at Preset Times Can Create Pitch

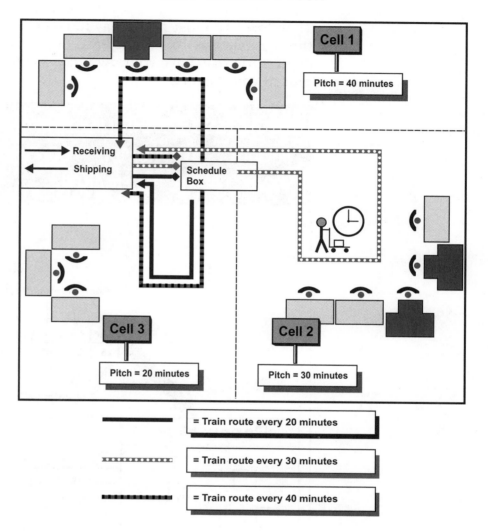

▬▬▬▬▬	= Train route every 20 minutes
✕✕✕✕✕✕✕✕✕	= Train route every 30 minutes
■■■■■■■	= Train route every 40 minutes

LEVELING USING PITCH

Pitch also means *leveling the volume of work at the pacemaker*. We consistently provide the pacemaker with the same volume of work, and that volume is leveled by pitch increments. In this manner we "break up" the received orders into pitch quantities and issue these quantities to the pacemaker. A good target pitch increment is usually between 15 minutes and two hours.

Creating a physical pitch is not always an easy thing to do, especially in a mixed environment. However, it is extremely important to implement pitch in lean manufacturing, as it provides a visual method to see waste and the disipline to reduce it. Therefore, we must find a way to create pitch. We will work through one way to do it at EMC Supply, but there are many others. You may have your own idea as you implement this concept in your factory.

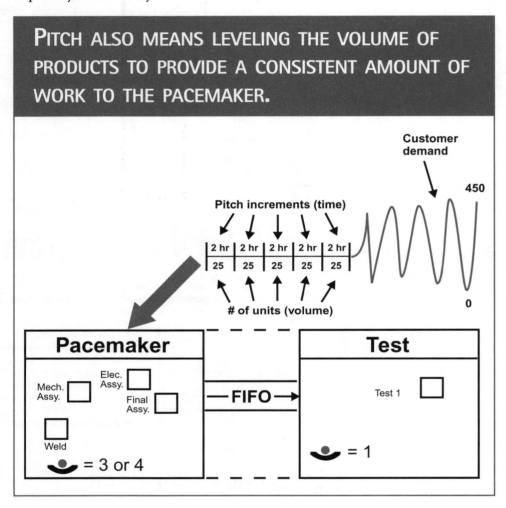

THE SCHEDULE BOX

It is always best when pitch increments are provided by some physical activity happening in the factory (just like people getting on the train—either they get on or they miss the train). A common way to achieve this is to have the material handler (the train) show up every pitch increment, take away the work completed, and provide the schedule for the next pitch increment. It is best if the work completed is a full box quantity or a pallet, so the cell would know it must produce a full box of parts every hour. To create pitch equal to a full box quantity, we multiply takt time by box quantity. Therefore, as a full box or pallet is produced, the material handler comes to take it away. Either it is done on time, or it is not. If it is not, then we ask why, and we usually ask it at least five times as part of the problem-solving process.

To visually incorporate pitch in the factory, we can introduce a visual scheduling system for the pacemaker. This is done by creating a *schedule box* and placing it near the cell. The schedule box can come in many different forms depending upon the application. If case pack quantities divide evenly into pitch increments a "post office box" type of schedule can be used. This box may look similar to mail slots used to sort mail. Cards will represent what products will be built during what pitch increments. A post office type schedule box is shown on the next page.

Post Office Box Scheduling Board

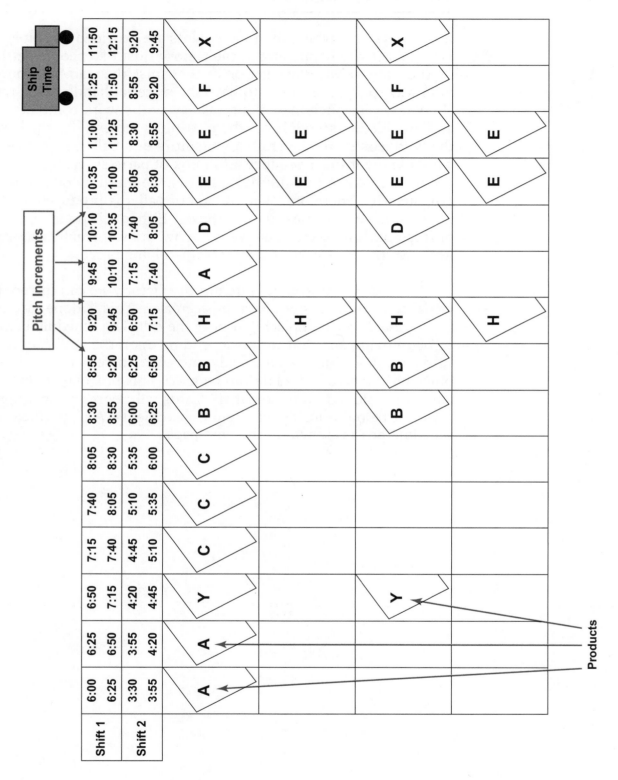

If the product family is small and only a few different mixes present themselves, a card rack with replaceable timelines may be used. Each slot in the rack can represent an increment of time. Replaceable time strips for the different mixes (these may also be preset for different mixes that reoccur) can be used to quickly adjust timelines for different mixes. Simply change the timeline each interval. Timeline boards can be stored on or near the rack for quick replacement.

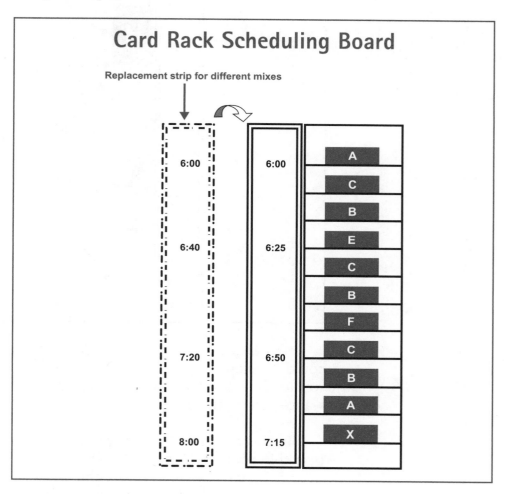

If the case pack quantities do not divide evenly into pitch increments, a *floating pitch board* can be used. A simple method to create one is to use a timeline with magnetic stickers that can be applied to it. Each sticker is sized to represent the amount of time it takes to produce a case (or perhaps a piece or a pallet). Products are loaded on the timeline magnetically at each interval. The material handler takes away the product and looks at the timeline to determine the next time they are needed. They can set a small timer (clipped to themselves) to remind them to show up at the appropriate time.

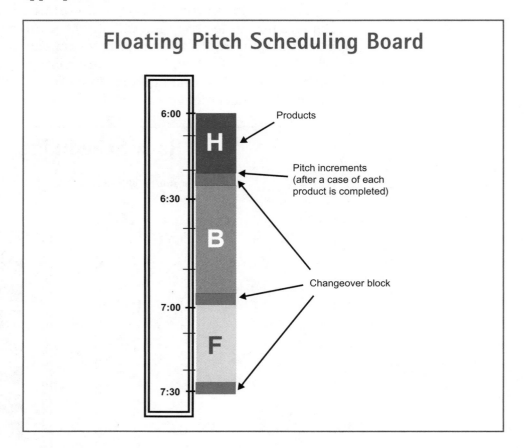

At EMC, we took a quick look at the products to see if we could develop the post office type of schedule box. This type would allow for consistent material routes in the factory, so we wanted to try this first.

In this schedule box, the pitch increment represents time slots placed in columns. Since there are multiple case packs in the product family, we have to consider this in the design of our schedule box. We will *subdivide each column* to allow for a mix of products to be made within each pitch increment. To determine how to subdivide each pitch increment, try and find a lowest common denominator for pack-out (case pack) quantities. Dividing the lowest common denominator (lowest common case pack quantity) into the pitch increment will tell us how many subdivisions are needed. For example, if some products have two per case, while others have four and eight per case, respectively, then our lowest common denominator is two, and four subdivisions are needed (8/2 = 4). This may require some work. We may have to adjust the pitch increment to provide an even number of subdivisions. Remember, with a takt time of two minutes, a good target pitch increment would be between 15 minutes and two hours.

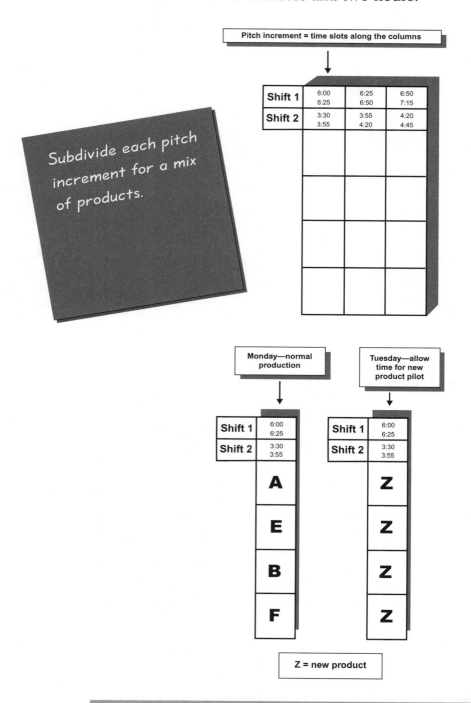

We can also allow for new products by placing cards into the time slots needed to run the new products.

CREATING PITCH AT EMC SUPPLY

Let's take a look at products built in the Arms & Pistons product family at EMC. This product family has a takt time of two minutes. Although we balanced work to a cycle time of 110 seconds, there is still variation in the process. Therefore, we will base our times on takt time, as that is when we will expect the work to be completed.

For each product in the family we determine the time to produce one case at takt time. Pack quantity is the amount of product packed in one case. The following table illustrates our findings at EMC Supply.

Product Code	Product Name	Pack Quantity	Takt Time	Time to Produce One Case
A	Sensor-Activated Arm	6	2 min	12 min
B	Laser-Activated Arm	6	2 min	12 min
C	Manually Activated Arm	6	2 min	12 min
D	Barcode Diverter Piston	6	2 min	12 min
E	Barcode Diverter Arm	12	2 min	24 min
F	Sensor-Activated Piston	12	2 min	24 min
G	Laser-Activated Piston	3	2 min	6 min
H	Manually Activated Piston	3	2 min	6 min

From this table we select the pitch increment. In a mixed environment, the pitch increment cannot be smaller than the longest time to produce one box or case of an item within the family. In this case the minimum pitch increment is equal to one case of product E or F, or 24 minutes. (Note: If we wanted a longer pitch increment, we would add two of product C, for a total of 48 minutes). By dividing the selected pitch increment by the time it takes to produce one case of the remaining products, we can establish the subdivisions and what mix of products can be built within the pitch increment.

Product Code	Product Name	Pack Quantity	Takt Time	Time to Produce One Case	Qty. per Pitch Increment
A	Sensor-Activated Arm	6	2 min	12 min	2
B	Laser-Activated Arm	6	2 min	12 min	2
C	Manually Activated Arm	6	2 min	12 min	2
D	Barcode Diverter Piston	6	2 min	12 min	2
E	Barcode Diverter Arm	12	2 min	24 min	1
F	Sensor-Activated Piston	12	2 min	24 min	1
G	Laser-Activated Piston	3	2 min	6 min	4
H	Manually Activated Piston	3	2 min	6 min	4

In this case, within 24 minutes, we could produce one case of product E or F, two cases of product A or B or C, or four cases of product G or H. We could also produce any mix of these products as long as the time to produce the mix added up to 24 minutes. As we mentioned earlier, changeovers are quick at this pacemaker (under 30 seconds). We will add 1 minute to each pitch increment to allow for changeovers and monitor the pacemaker performance. This will yield a pitch time at EMC Supply of 25 minutes.

In effect, each pitch increment is a "bucket of capacity" that is open for production control to schedule. It doesn't matter which products go in the pitch increment, the time to produce should always add up to a constant, standard pitch increment. At the end of each pitch increment, the material handler hands out the schedule for the next pitch (which may be a combination of products) and takes away the completed pitch increment of work.

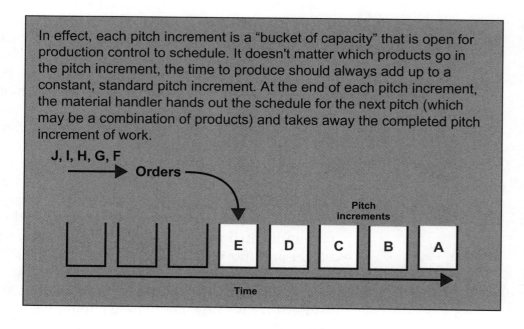

The resulting layout of the schedule box is as follows.

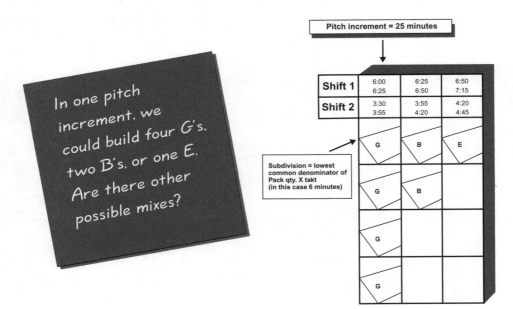

If pack quantities do not have a common denominator, the first question should be, "Can we change the pack size?" (see pp. 123–124). It may take a little work, but having common pack sizes within the same value stream of mixed products will greatly help synchronize the factory to customer demand. The ability to change pack size often depends on why the original pack size was chosen to begin with. Was it based on customer demand? On investigation, we often find that there is no logical reason for the pack size to be the way it is. Perhaps the sizing was set the way it is to optimize material handling or logistics. Remember, optimize packaging for ease of use in the cell first, and then consider material handling. We want the cell to be operating with minimal waste.

However, if pack quantities cannot be changed, we have to find other ways to create pitch. If full case quantities do not yield a common pitch increment, we could have the material handler take individual units (instead of full cases) away from the pacemaker and move these to the next process. What is important is that the material handler still needs to show up at regular intervals. A visual method must be developed to answer the questions, "Where are we now and where should we be now?" Using the material handler is a good way to provide this information.

EMC Supply's Schedule Box

Each pitch increment represents 25 minutes of time.
Within each pitch incement, a mix of products can be built.

Ship Time

	6:00	6:25	6:50	7:15	7:40	8:05	8:30	8:55	9:20	9:45	10:10	10:35	11:00	11:25	11:50
Shift 1	6:25	6:50	7:15	7:40	8:05	8:30	8:55	9:20	9:45	10:10	10:35	11:00	11:25	11:50	12:15
Shift 2	3:30	3:55	4:20	4:45	5:10	5:35	6:00	6:25	6:50	7:15	7:40	8:05	8:30	8:55	9:20
	3:55	4:20	4:45	5:10	5:35	6:00	6:25	6:50	7:15	7:40	8:05	8:30	8:55	9:20	9:45

Remember, using multiple product cards increases the ability to lose them! There's nothing worse than a lost kanban card. Be sure to work with employees to develop and implement the system, so everyone will understand and maintain it.

Pitch is always created at the pacemaker process. From this, process work will flow in a continuous fashion to shipping. At EMC Supply, the schedule box will provide instructions for the pacemaker (welding and assembly cell). Work will flow into the testing FIFO lane at each pitch increment. Work will flow out of testing at a varying rate, averaging around 110 seconds based on the mix. Therefore, we will need a FIFO lane after testing to absorb this variation. The material handler (or perhaps the operator in this case, since testing is in the cell area) should move work into the FIFO lane at each pitch increment, then check to see if the FIFO lane, after testing, has enough product to be moved into shipping.

The key to maintaining good pitch at the pacemaker in a mixed environment is to have each product balanced to a consistent cycle time. With a good balance, it won't matter what product is made or what the mix is, something will always come out each takt time, which will allow for steady paced withdrawal from the pacemaker at the pitch increment. The key to consistent cycle times is the development of standard work. *Good standard work practices will drive the variation out of the cycle time.*

INVERSE PITCH

Sometimes takt times are so long (four hours or greater) that our pitch increment may need to be shorter than our takt time. In these cases we call this *inverse pitch*. We still need to have a pitch increment a few times per day, even though our product may be built at the rate of once per week. We should try to target a minimum of four pitch increments per shift, as this will let us know where we are four times before the shift ends. We will have to be creative when working in inverse pitch as it is not always easy to provide small chunks of work when building large products that require days or months to build.

How would you handle the situation where takt time is six hours? How do you break up the work and give workers a management timeframe?

Option one: Break the work down into an "assembly line" fashion, with the work being completed in small chunks. The operator then moves it to another station and continues to work on it.

Option two: Computer screen—have the standard work broken into chunks and make the operator validate each time a chunk is completed on the computer. Lights display the status: green = on schedule, yellow = behind, blue = ahead, red = critically behind.

Option three: Provide enough component parts to last only one pitch increment. More parts are delivered on the next pitch increment and the previous supply should be empty, or we are behind.

Option four: Moving assembly—paint a line on the floor that shows the halfway point. If the operator hasn't done half the work on reaching the halfway point, the yellow light goes on; red goes on if half the work is not done by the end of the takt time.

Option five: Create FIFO lanes with quantity and progress arrows suspended above the lane.

Option six: You may have your own idea!

THE FUTURE STATE

Now that we have selected a product family, determined takt, balanced our flow, created standard work, and established pitch, we are once again ready to update our future state, so it's back to the whiteboard.

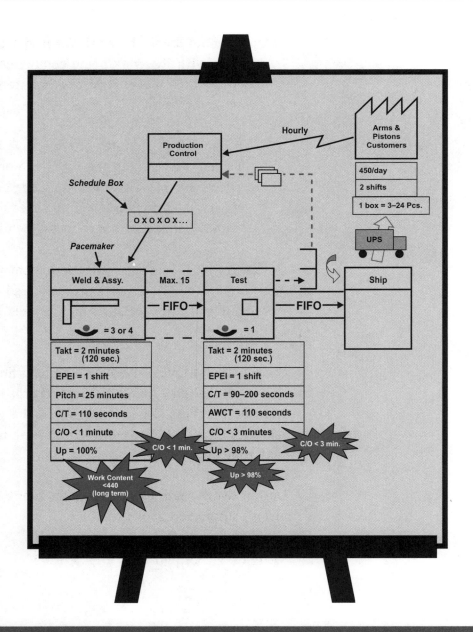

Summary

Creating a pitch increment at the pacemaker can be challenging. It may even involve resizing pack quantities to even things out. Using multiples of the largest pack quantity will simplify pitch at the pacemaker, as a mix of other products in the family can be produced within this time. When this is not feasible, or long takt times exist, you may have to find a way to indicate visually, at regular intervals, the current production status and time increment. All workers should be able to see the visual indicator from their station, and when the pitch increment is not met they must ask why.

What Have We Done So Far with the EMC Team?

We have now discussed with the team how to develop pitch at the pacemaker. This included:

- ❏ Designing the schedule box
- ❏ Calculating common denominators for different case pack quantities
- ❏ Calculating pitch based on different case quantities
- ❏ Determining the subdivisions needed for the schedule box

This completes our pacemaker design. It will require some effort and discipline for EMC to implement. However, the concepts are easy to teach and EMC management feels their people will understand and want to try working with a smaller management time frame. We reminded them that the key is to get the operators involved in problem solving immediately when the pitch increment is not obtained. This will provide ownership and culture change, which is needed to ensure success.

What's Next for the Team?

Now that our pacemaker design is complete, we will move to the leveling loop. (See p. 134; for a larger version see the accompanying CD.) Our next step it to determine with the team how to schedule the pacemaker. We need to cover:

- ❏ Performing a mix analysis
- ❏ Creating logic charts
- ❏ Loading the schedule box

The team reminded us that their scheduling and on-time delivery needs improvement and any help we can give in this area would be greatly appreciated. We were very pleased with their enthusiasm, as we will be teaching them new concepts for scheduling that are very different from those they are currently using.

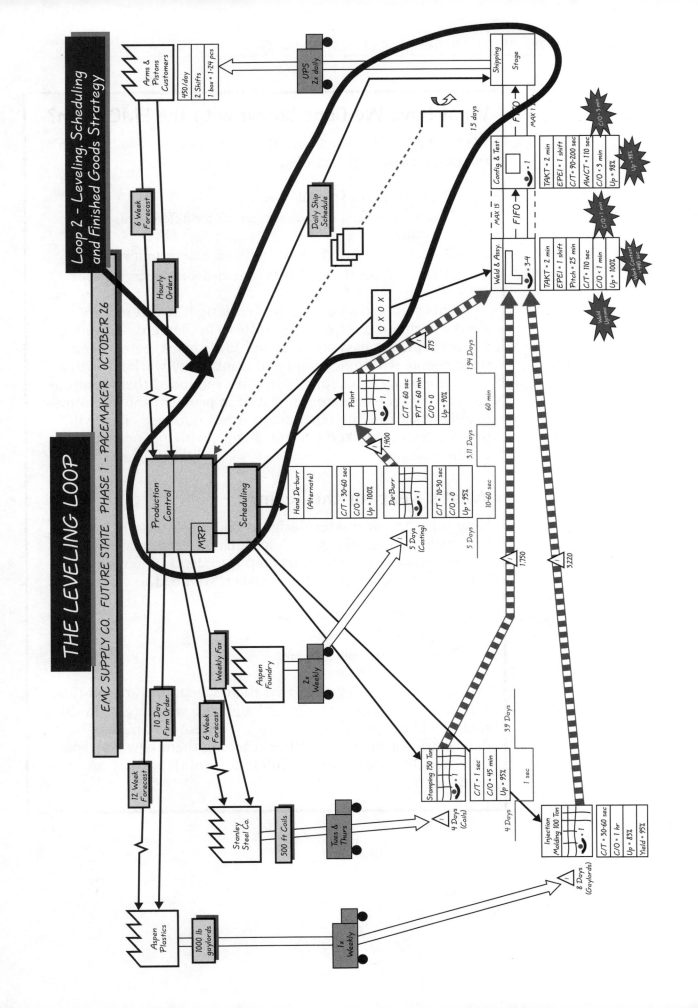

QUESTION 9—

How Will We Schedule the Mix at the Pacemaker?

When scheduling the pacemaker, we know that smaller increments are better. As discussed previously, smaller increments provide us with better quality, smoother flow through shared resources, and higher flexibility to the customer (see p. 64). Small increments also require nearly zero changeover time and perfect quality at the pacemaker.

Scheduling the pacemaker (and the value stream) would be easy if every product had exactly the same work content and cycle times. If this were true, we could build practically any mix, as the time would be the same for all products. However, a high mix of products with high machine cycles is more difficult to build. Therefore, we need to review the pacemaker and the value stream for variations in cycle time, as some mix variations may not be able to meet demand within the interval.

Before we schedule our mix at the pacemaker, we need to understand the limits of the value stream in regard to various mixes. We will start by testing the limits of the pacemaker. After this, we may need to check other processes in the value stream to see if they will restrict the mix.

Sample Value Stream

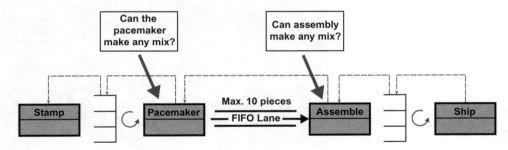

At EMC Supply, production control must manage three sources of orders. Orders are received to refill the supermarket through kanban cards; custom orders are processed and issued by engineering; and customers phone, fax, or send their orders through the Internet.

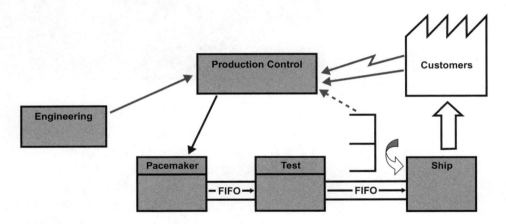

Production control will do its best to build to demand each day and ship what is ordered each day. However, we know there will be peaks and valleys in customer demand, so we will place some finished goods of regular-selling items in a supermarket and pull from this when demand is high. When demand is low, we will replenish the supermarket.

As we discussed in balancing flow, if a product has high labor content, we have the option of adding labor and workstations when that product is run (see pp. 98–99). But if a product has a high machine time, it may be difficult for us to add machines when that product is run. In this case we may have to *limit the mix* to allow only so many of these products to be built per day, carrying more finished goods to cover peaks. If we don't do so, we might be unable to build every other product needed that day.

When we build a high mix of product through the same value stream, we strive to build what the customer wants each day with the least amount of waste. However, the value stream has limits. Therefore, we may still have to perform some leveling with finished goods, or work overtime until all orders are shipped each day.

With a wide variety of orders coming in each day, *production control needs to determine the limits of the pacemaker in terms of mix variety and volume*. In order to do this, we need to perform a *mix analysis*.

In the mix analysis we first look at the pacemaker in terms of machine cycle time to see if there are any bottlenecks (a bottleneck is a process that cannot meet takt time). We check machines first, as it may be difficult to change machine cycle times. We can add operators if labor causes the bottleneck. At EMC Supply, the pacemaker consists mostly of assembly, with machines being used for welding. Since welding has a very small machine cycle compared to the takt time, we will skip the details of welding and look at the entire pacemaker for our analysis.

Therefore, we will perform our mix analysis in two areas: the pacemaker and testing. To begin, we will set up a table that shows the anticipated mix, the takt time for the pacemaker, and the cycle times at testing.

Mix Analysis
Pacemaker takt = 120 seconds

Product Code	Product Name	Pacemaker Takt Time	Testing Cycle Time	Anticipated Mix
A	Sensor-Activated Arm	120	110 sec	65
B	Laser-Activated Arm	120	110 sec	85
C	Manually Activated Arm	120	100 sec	35
D	Barcode Diverter Piston	120	110 sec	70
E	Barcode Diverter Arm	120	105 sec	50
F	Sensor-Activated Piston	120	90 sec	55
G	Laser-Activated Piston	120	200 sec	20
H	Manually Activated Piston	120	100 sec	25
X	Custom Orders	120	110 sec	45
TOTAL: 450 units per day				

The laser-activated piston (product G) has a test cycle time of 200 seconds. With a takt time of two minutes, EMC cannot produce this item to takt time. Therefore, we need to limit the mix of this item in order to have time to build other products.

Another method to review the limits of the mix is to determine the maximum volume by product. For any product that is

> *For any product that is over takt time we need to ask, "How many can we produce if customers order this product only?"*

over takt time we need to ask: *"How many can we produce if customers order this product only?"* We can determine this by dividing the available minutes per interval by the work content and machine times, respectively.

Since we chose the option of adding labor on the high work content products (products D and G), we know the pacemaker can always perform at takt. However, product G exceeds takt at the testing station. We could add more machines, but this can be expensive (as with EMC Supply), and is not always our first choice. Instead, we have placed a small FIFO lane to balance the pacemaker with testing. The FIFO lane also allows us to gain back time on the products with test cycles that are faster than the pacemaker takt.

Pacemaker takt = 120 seconds

Product Code	Product Name	Pacemaker Takt Time	Testing Cycle Time	Available Minutes (2 shifts)	Max Mix Limit
A	Sensor-Activated Arm	120 sec	110 sec	900 min	450
B	Laser-Activated Arm	120 sec	110 sec	900 min	450
C	Manually Activated Arm	120 sec	100 sec	900 min	450
D	Barcode Diverter Piston	120 sec	110 sec	900 min	450
E	Barcode Diverter Arm	120 sec	105 sec	900 min	450
F	Sensor-Activated Piston	120 sec	90 sec	900 min	450
G	Laser-Activated Piston	120 sec	200 sec	900 min	**270**
H	Manually Activated Piston	120 sec	100 sec	900 min	450
X	Custom Orders	120 sec	110 sec	900 min	450

We may be able to increase the available hours on testing (i.e., work overtime) depending upon the mix to finish the FIFO inventory each shift. At the end of each shift, all orders should be complete and no inventory should be left in the FIFO lane.

In order to keep the FIFO lane from becoming just an inventory pile and growing beyond the interval, we would also limit the number of product G that we build in succession. We would only allow so many of product G to be "sprinkled in" each interval. To determine the mix limits of the test station and how many of product G we can add, we will develop a *mix logic chart*.

MIX LOGIC CHARTS

> **Mix logic charts may only be needed when there are products that exceed takt time in the value stream. If all products are within 30 percent of work content, you might be okay!**

Mix logic charts are built upon a series of yes/no questions that lead us through decision making. They allow us to know quickly if we need to revise a mix, work overtime, or pull from the supermarket. The mix logic chart tells us how to balance orders against today's load. It can be used by production control or by the material handler who is loading the schedule box.

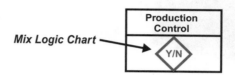

The mix logic chart can be created in a flowchart format. It will contain logic, questions, and decision points. Each decision must be answered yes or no. Based on the answers, a path will be followed. At the end of each path, an action is suggested. For example, on days where the customer's orders exceed 450 units, a question might be: "Is there enough inventory in the supermarket to cover the balance?" If the answer is yes, the action might be to level and build the mix. If the answer is no, we continue on to the next question.

Constructing the Mix Logic Chart

Each mix logic chart must be developed for a specific value stream. The charts may vary widely in size and complexity, but there are some basic ground rules that apply to the construction of any mix logic chart:

- ❐ All questions asked on the chart must be answered yes or no.
- ❐ All ending points must relay specific action to be taken.
- ❐ The chart must provide standard actions that your company has agreed upon for each yes/no response.

A typical mix logic chart would contain questions such as those shown on the next page.

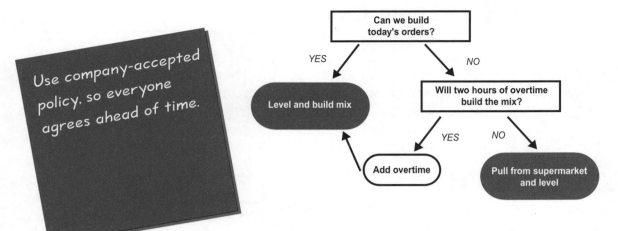

Although many variables enter into the development of each chart, some basic steps are common to the construction of any mix logic chart:

Step 1: Identify commodity items.

Step 2: Determine which part at which process cannot meet takt time.

Step 3: Calculate the total time needed for this part of the process.

Step 4: Determine remaining time to build other products at this process.

Step 5: Determine quantity to pull from supermarket or overtime work needed to make today's orders.

Step 6: If demand is low on the other products, determine how many products could be built back into the supermarket.

You may need to develop further questions based on your product family and company culture. These might include: "Is there more than one product that limits the mix?" and "Will working two hours of overtime build the mix?"

Remember, the outcome of the mix logic chart is to suggest action. Make sure each path ends with an action item. Avoid action items like: "See the production control supervisor," or "Use your discretion." These answers may end in a response such as "Let's make an exception today," and ultimately we will be making exceptions every day. If the mix logic chart is not providing the right actions, *correct it*.

CREATING THE MIX LOGIC CHART AT EMC SUPPLY

We know we have balanced the pacemaker to produce any product in two minutes, but the testing station has a product that exceeds takt. We give the schedule to the pacemaker, but we must make sure we can get the work through the testing station. We will use a mix logic chart that checks the mix at the testing station each day.

As we mentioned earlier, production control manages three sources of information for orders. Actual customer orders, custom orders that have been approved by engineering, and kanban cards from the supermarket (from products that were shipped at the end of the day). Production control wants to build actual customer orders and the custom orders each day, using commodity items in the supermarket to balance the overflow. Product G is not a commodity item, and they do not keep any in the supermarket. Therefore, product G is always built when ordered. Other products can be pulled from the supermarket to cover any lost time. Any time left over (such as when demand is lower) is used to replenish commodity items in the finished-goods supermarket.

We did not put all the details into the chart on the next page, as they can be quite involved. Instead, we provided a good starting point, just to get a feel for the concept.

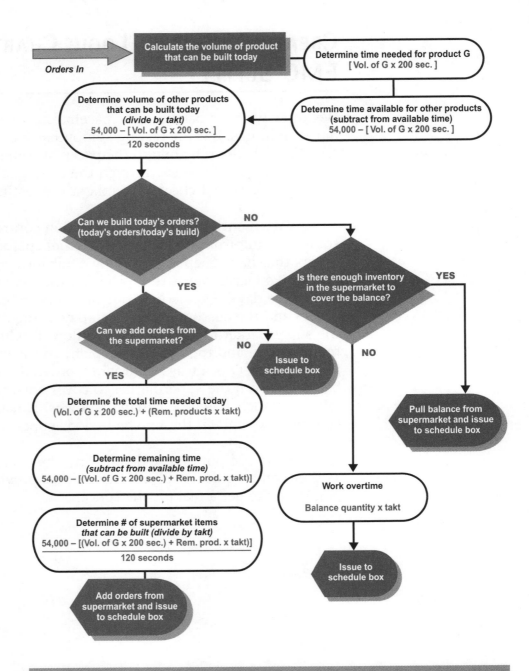

In most cases we look from the pacemaker forward to the customer and assume that the shared resources (equipment that is shared across multiple product families) have inventory in the supermarkets to buffer against fluctuations. However, shared resources also are limited to what they can produce each interval, so it may be a good idea to check the mix against them as well.

Applying the Mix Logic Chart to EMC's Orders

For Monday's orders, the product family total demand is lower than anticipated. However, orders for product G total 36 units, which is higher than the anticipated mix of 20 and exceed our AWCT (p. 86). In this case we may be able to build more than 20, but we are not sure if we can build all 39 units *and* the remaining orders. We need to determine if we can make this mix, pull from inventory, or work overtime.

Product Code	Product Name	Pack Quantity	Anticipated Demand	Total Orders (pieces)
A	Sensor-Activated Arm	6	65	42
B	Laser-Activated Arm	6	85	48
C	Manually Activated Arm	6	35	24
D	Barcode Diverter Piston	6	70	66
E	Barcode Diverter Arm	12	50	72
F	Sensor-Activated Piston	12	55	60
H	Manually Activated Piston	3	25	54
X	Custom Orders	3	45	36
		Totals	**430**	**402**
G	Laser-Activated Piston (limit 20)	3	20	36

Total for Monday: 438 units

Follow the arrows on the next page to track this mix through the mix logic chart. ⟶

After reviewing the mix logic chart on the next page, you can see that in this case the supermarket was low on inventory and already at the reorder point. Therefore, we needed to work overtime in order to get out the day's orders. Most likely, tomorrow's orders will be lower for product G and we will replenish the supermarket.

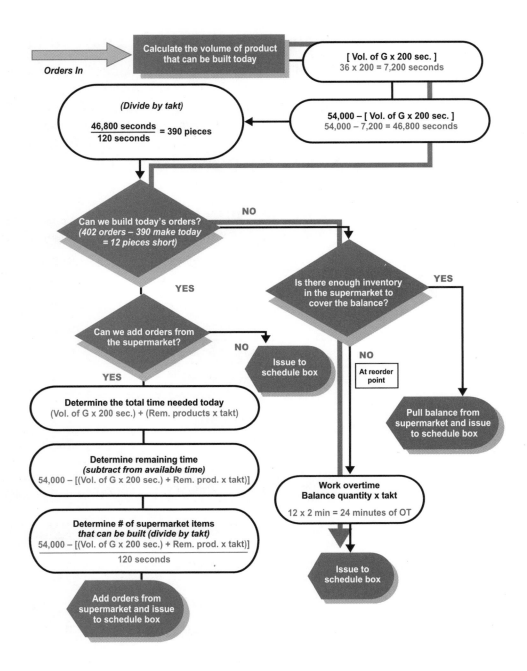

Orders In

Calculate the volume of product that can be built today

[Vol. of G x 200 sec.]
36 x 200 = 7,200 seconds

(Divide by takt)

$$\frac{46,800 \text{ seconds}}{120 \text{ seconds}} = 390 \text{ pieces}$$

54,000 – [Vol. of G x 200 sec.]
54,000 – 7,200 = 46,800 seconds

Can we build today's orders?
*(402 orders – 390 make today
= 12 pieces short)*

NO

Is there enough inventory
in the supermarket to
cover the balance?

YES

YES

Can we add orders from
the supermarket?

NO

Issue to
schedule box

NO

At reorder
point

YES

YES

Determine the total time needed today
(Vol. of G x 200 sec.) + (Rem. products x takt)

Pull balance from
supermarket and issue
to schedule box

Determine remaining time
(subtract from available time)
54,000 – [(Vol. of G x 200 sec.) + Rem. prod. x takt)]

Work overtime
Balance quantity x takt

12 x 2 min = 24 minutes of OT

Determine # of supermarket items
that can be built (divide by takt)
$$\frac{54,000 - [(\text{Vol. of G x 200 sec.}) + \text{Rem. prod. x takt})]}{120 \text{ seconds}}$$

Issue to
schedule box

Add orders from
supermarket and issue
to schedule box

LEVELING THE MIX

Now that we know how to balance today's mix with what we can build at each interval, the next step is to populate the schedule box to level the mix within the interval.

At EMC Supply, we determined our interval was one shift. This means we want to level the mix to build every product on an interval of one shift. On the schedule box the interval should be clearly indicated. If we ship more than twice a day, then the schedule box should have indicators locating these points.

When trying to determine what point to level to, common questions are: *Should we level to more than one interval per day if we only ship once per day? Are there benefits to this?* Absolutely. By building a small mix of many products, quality problems can easily be found and corrected, with only a very small amount of inventory affected. Less space is needed, and tracking of WIP inventory is greatly reduced if not eliminated. Small lots of mixed products develop a culture where operators recognize that high flexibility to produce what customers want, when they want it, with very little waste, is the key to successful business growth.

Small lots prevent waste from slipping in. *The larger the lot size, the more chance for waste to creep in.* Small lots provide high discipline for quick changeovers and maintaining takt image or management timeframe. Small lots also allow you to fill small orders, not just sizable orders (and thereby possibly penetrate new markets). Even if

Advantages of intervals that are smaller than the ship window:

- Eliminate quality problems before they grow.
- Provide no opportunity for waste.
- Use less space.
- Reduce inventory tracking.
- Change culture to eliminate waste.
- Provide discipline for quick change and pitch.
- Allow small orders to be met equally with large orders.
- Provide smooth flow through shared resources as small quantities are needed versus large batches.

Smaller intervals require more frequent trips by material handlers, so everything must be close together!

---

1. *Learning to See*. Mike Rother and John Shook. The Lean Enterprise Institute, 1999, p.51.

your ship window is once a week, it is best to cycle through every product in small mixed lots in as little time as possible.

LOADING THE SCHEDULE BOX

We have previously decided that EMC Supply could run this product family at an interval of one shift. This means we can only run each product once per shift until we improve changeover times. How do we determine what order will fill the schedule box?

Since it would be difficult to vary the labor at each pitch increment of the pacemaker, we may need to produce those products with the same number of operators together. As we recall from the balancing flow section (p. 101), the labor required was as follows.

3 OPERATORS		4 OPERATORS	
Product Code	Product Name	Product Code	Product Name
A	Sensor-Activated Arm	D	Barcode Diverter Piston
B	Laser-Activated Arm	G	Laser-Activated Piston
C	Manually Activated Arm		
E	Barcode Diverter Arm		
F	Sensor-Activated Piston		
H	Manually Activated Piston		

Therefore we would choose to run products D and G together, either at the beginning or the end of the shift. Since we always want work ready for the tester in the FIFO lane, we should always start the shift with product G, as it has the longest test time. This will allow products with quick test cycles to accumulate in the FIFO lane and be ready as soon as testing is complete.

A method to simplify loading the schedule box is to color code the cards by time needed. Those products that require a full pitch increment can be a solid dark color, while those requiring only a portion of the pitch increment can be a light color.

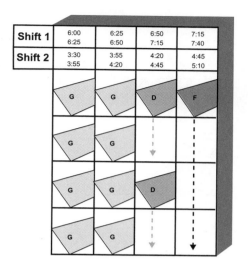

Shift 1	6:00 6:25	6:25 6:50	6:50 7:15	7:15 7:40
Shift 2	3:30 3:55	3:55 4:20	4:20 4:45	4:45 5:10

Let's review Monday's orders and see how we would populate the schedule box.

Product Code	Product Name	Pack Qty.	Monday's Orders			
			Total Orders (pieces)	Total Orders (cases)	1st Shift	2nd Shift
A	Sensor-Activated Arm	6	42	7	4	3
B	Laser-Activated Arm	6	48	8	4	4
C	Manually Activated Arm	6	24	4	2	2
D	Barcode Diverter Piston	6	66	11	5	6
E	Barcode Diverter Arm	12	72	6	3	3
F	Sensor-Activated Piston	12	60	5	3	2
G	Laser-Activated Piston	3	36	12	6	6
H	Manually Activated Piston	3	54	18	9	9
X	Custom Orders	3	36	12	6	6

First, we will load the cards for products G and D, as these will require four operators. Then we will load the remaining products, as they only require three operators.

It may be a good idea to place a digital clock with large numbers on the schedule box. This may avoid people asking: "Whose watch do we use?"

6:00

Shift 1	6:00 / 6:25	6:25 / 6:50	6:50 / 7:15	7:15 / 7:40	7:40 / 8:05	8:05 / 8:30	8:40 / 9:05	9:05 / 9:30	9:30 / 9:55	9:55 / 10:20	10:20 / 10:45	10:45 / 11:10	11:40 / 12:05	12:05 / 12:30	12:30 / 12:55	1:05 / 1:30	1:30 / 1:55	1:55 / 2:20	2:20 / 2:30
	G	G	G	D	F	F	F	E	E	E	B	B	C	A	A	H	H	H	X
	G	G	G													H	H	X	X
	D	D	D	D							B	B	C	A	A	H	H	X	X
																H	H	X	

4 Operators   **3 Operators**

A Word about Machine Cells

In some factories (such as machine shops) we cannot balance the cycle times of all the products in the family to the takt time. We cannot add labor to insure that all products will run through the pacemaker at the same speed. Cycle times in a machine cell may be fixed, and not every product will have the same cycle time. Some products may take longer to build than others. To stabilize flow through the pacemaker and shared resources, we have to determine a pattern that optimizes flow through the machine cell. Selecting a pattern depends upon factors such as setup, tooling and fixtures needed, material presentation, and other concerns.

One pattern would be to build from low cycle-time products to high cycle-time products, then steadily back to low cycle-time products. Think of it as climbing up and down stairs. You climb up the stairs (to the high cycle-time products) then back down the stairs (to the low cycle-time products) at the same rate. This has a cyclic effect like the pacemaker and can smooth out pulses or spikes through the factory.

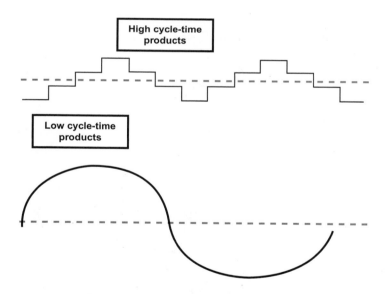

In a machine shop environment, the kanban cards should also be color-coded. This allows us to view the flow through the pacemaker visually and helps us identify difficult mixes ahead of time. Another aspect of a correctly loaded schedule box may be color-coded cards placed in a repeated pattern that resembles repeating rainbows—this is very easy to teach!

THE FUTURE STATE

We are getting close to completing our mixed model future state.
We once again update the whiteboard to show our progress.

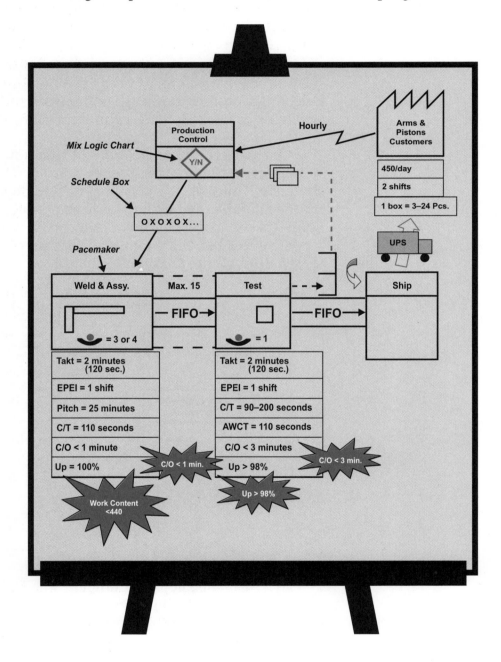

Summary

Although we target the ability to make any mix of the product family through the value stream, we must check the value stream to ensure that extents of possible mixes are obtainable. Since some machine cycles are longer than others, a high volume of longer-cycle products could prevent all the products that are needed from being built on time. In order to check for these conditions, we use a mix analysis and a mix logic chart. The analysis tells us which products we may need to limit. The chart provides us with a binary decision process to determine what can be built at each interval, knowing the limitations of the possible mixes.

What Have We Done So Far with the EMC Team?

We have now discussed with the team how to schedule various mixes through their value stream. This included:

- ❏ Using a mix analysis to determine potential bottlenecks
- ❏ Using mix logic charts to level production at pacemaker
- ❏ Loading the schedule box based on mix and labor

The team has learned that using mix logic charts to provide a consistent scheduling method, along with a scheduling box on the shopfloor, ties together the concepts of mixed model production at the pacemaker. Their enthusiasm for getting started is showing, as they now see how a lean system can be applied to their high-mix environment.

What's Next for the Team?

Although the group is eager to start implementation, we still need to discuss one more factor. Even though we have made a highly flexible value stream that can handle a range of mixes, customer demand for the entire family can still increase beyond what the value stream can handle. Therefore, we must review with the team:

- ❏ Flexing the pacemaker with different takt times
- ❏ Smoothing demand with dynamic supermarkets
- ❏ Sizing and refining finished good supermarkets

PART V:
CUSTOMER DEMAND

❑ **Question 10—How Will We Deal with Changes in Customer Demand?**

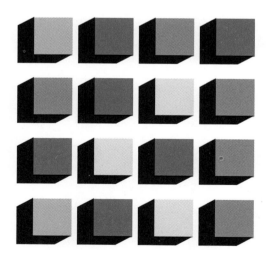

QUESTION 10—
How Will We Deal with Changes in Customer Demand?

Our future state allows for a small finished-goods supermarket of commodity items to help smooth demand. As demand changes beyond what the supermarket can absorb, we can add another shift (or additional stations) and rebalance the cell to a new takt time.

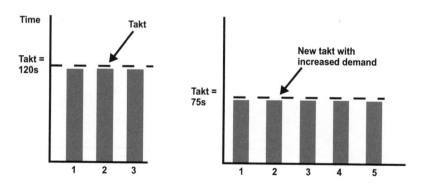

We can also vary the output of the cell by varying the number of operators in it. For example, if demand is down for a day, we may not have to add operators when products G and D are built. Instead, we may let the pacemaker run slower. In effect, we can set different modes of output for the pacemaker based on demand and the resources available. These modes should be preset so that everyone knows in what mode the cell will operate and under what conditions (a logic chart similar to the mix logic chart can help here).

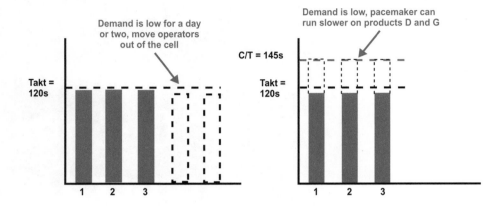

If the demand trends begin to change and exceed what we can produce, even with the help of the supermarket, we may also have to add equipment (at EMC Supply, another tester) or another shift. However, as this option may be expensive and may have to be put into effect quickly, it may not be practical. Therefore, many companies level the amount of production for a fixed period of time, usually three months.

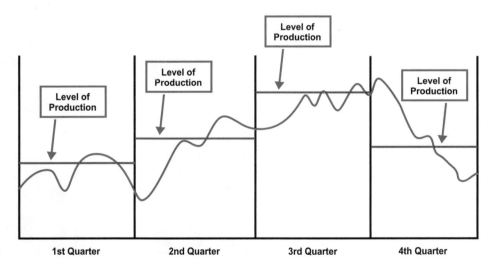

Is there a good method for forecasting demand? Many manufacturers will say no, and we tend to agree. It seems there is no crystal ball that can predict what customers will need months from now. Many manufacturing sites state: "If sales gives us an accurate forecast, we can build everything the customer wants on time." This would seem to be a true statement. However, we may get a different perspective on manufacturing if we ask: "Why can't sales provide us with a good forecast?"

As we mentioned to the team when we first began: The shorter the lead time, the more accurate the forecast.

SMOOTHING DEMAND WITH DYNAMIC SUPERMARKETS

While it may be impractical to try to build exactly to demand, we can try to match it more closely by dividing the demand into small intervals and creating a dynamic finished-goods supermarket that changes based on demand signals.

To make the supermarket dynamic, we may put in a system that alters the supermarket size in line with demand changes. This will prevent us from falling short on customer orders when demand trends exceed our future-state design. We will need to look forward to anticipated demand—but not in terms of a long-term forecast.

A finished-goods supermarket absorbs variation in customer demand. The question becomes, "How much should we absorb?" Extra inventory is waste, and we don't want to overproduce. In most companies, sales and marketing tries to set inventory levels based on the forecast, while plant management sets inventory levels to try to improve productivity and efficiency. The real answer comes down to lead time.

The shorter the lead time, the more flexible the value stream and the less inventory needed. The lead time through the value stream may identify a starting point for the finished-goods supermarket. In a high-mix environment we would ask: *How long will it take any part to travel from order to finished goods?* If it takes two days, then we may need to carry at least two days' worth of finished-goods inventory. If it takes four hours, then the inventory is at least four hours' worth of finished goods, which is significantly less. Lead time is directly related to EPEI. As illustrated earlier, the smaller the interval and the smaller the lead time, *the less chaos in the system.*

When deciding on a finished-goods strategy, a good method is to break demand into lead-time intervals. Then we change the finished-goods supermarket based on lead-time intervals.

Remember, we always need to look at total demand for the family rather than individual products. Our goal is to create different modes for the value stream that allow us to build to demand as much as possible throughout the year. Everyone should be aware of the different modes and which mode they are currently in. It may be a good idea to have a visual signal in the production control office specifying the current mode to get everyone on the same page quickly.

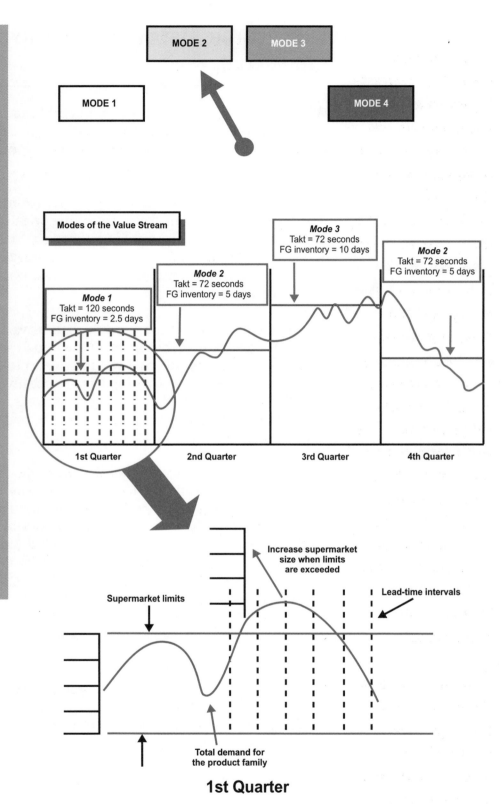

1st Quarter

We can establish preset levels of the supermarket inventory based on the flexibility and performance of the value stream, then signal changes to the supermarket similar to a kanban system. For example, if five lead time intervals from the present day demand exceeds what we can build, that will send a signal to increase the supermarket now and begin building immediately to the higher level. When the fifth interval is reached, we should have enough inventory to absorb the spike in demand.

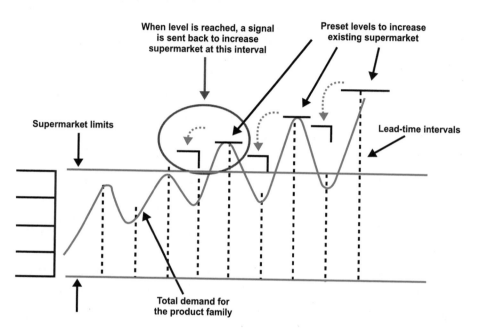

Implementing a dynamic finished-goods supermarket may not be as difficult as it seems. We simply need to rope off or block supermarket spaces when they are not needed in order to keep manufacturing from overproducing. Since the spaces are blocked, we also remove the corresponding kanban cards to prevent extra inventory from being built. The best way to make this system effective is to make it simple and visual.

At EMC Supply, we decided that we would try to build exactly to customer demand each day. When demand exceeds the value stream limit, we pull commodity items from the finished-goods supermarket to offset the excess demand. Each day production control places actual orders in the schedule box. If they have time left over, they replenish the supermarket.

DETERMINING THE STARTING POINT

The first step to establishing a finished-goods supermarket is to analyze the range of variation of each of the products in the family.

Prod. Code	Product Name	Anticipated Demand per Day	Range +/– %
A	Sensor-Activated Arm	65	35%
B	Laser-Activated Arm	85	50%
C	Manually Activated Arm	35	25%
D	Barcode Diverter Piston	70	10%
E	Barcode Diverter Arm	50	30%
F	Sensor-Activated Piston	55	25%
G	Laser-Activated Piston	20	10%
H	Manually Activated Piston	25	25%
X	Custom Orders	45	20%
	Total	450	Max. 50%

From this data, we decided we would start by keeping products A, B, and E in the supermarket, as they have the highest variation and are steady sellers. Since the variation of product B is 50 percent, two days of high orders could deplete our supermarket and make us fall short on orders. As a starting estimate, we will keep four days of product B, and three days of products A and E. This would total around 685 pieces, which is about one and a half days on inventory for the total family—enough to absorb the day-to-day variation. In fact, it is probably a little too much. We should monitor the amount carefully and strive to continuously reduce it.

A simple visual method to monitor our estimate is to place a removable marker, such as a card, cone, magnetic bar, or any device that can be removed (but not too easily) on each location in the supermarket. As a container is pulled from a supermarket location for the first time, remove the marker. Run this system for a few weeks and monitor it. If the supermarket is too large, you will find locations of inventory with the marker still remaining. Remove some of this inventory, shrink the supermarket, replace the markers, and try again.

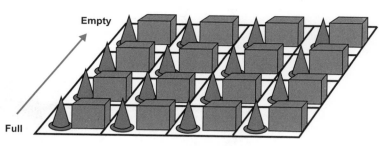

Original Supermarket Setup
Remove the cone when you use the location for the first time.

There is too much inventory in my supermarket!

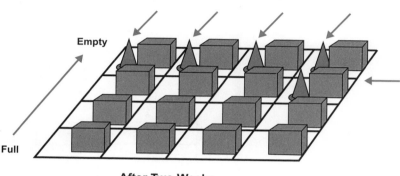

After Two Weeks
You do not need any locations where cones remain.

When we finished, we updated our future state with the lead time ladder (see p. 8). We constructed the ladder by starting at the pacemaker and working out to the customer. We did not go back through the upstream processes, as we had not worked on them yet. The team has already seen a significant improvement and is ready to move ahead.

THE FUTURE STATE

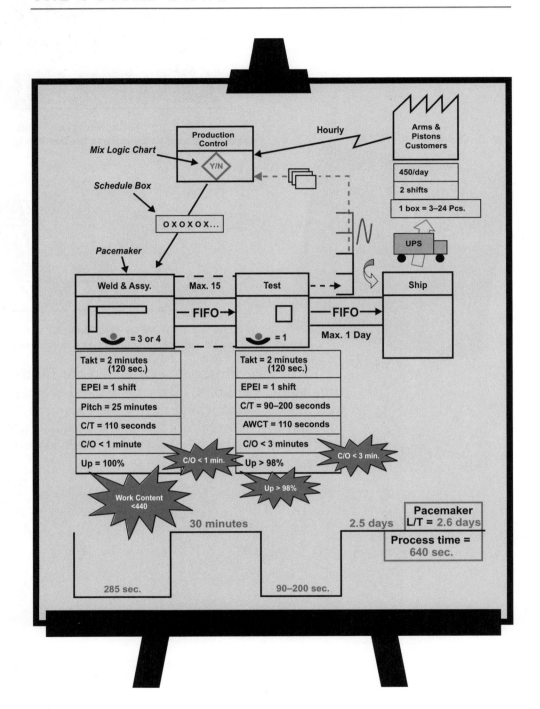

Summary

In a high-mix environment we must decide if we can build the anticipated mix at each interval. If we can't, our first choice is to further eliminate waste at the pacemaker. We may also choose to increase available hours at the pacemaker, or perhaps create another cell to offload pacemaker work. However, this may be difficult if demand fluctuations occur on a day-to-day basis.

If none of these options are available, we create a finished-goods supermarket to help us absorb demand variations. The finished-goods supermarket needs to be dynamic and expand with customer demand. It should also shrink as customer demand declines. The key to sizing the supermarket and deciding when it should grow and shrink is lead time. The smaller the lead time, the more variation is absorbed and the less inventory is needed.

What Have We Done So Far with the EMC Team?

At this point the lights seemed to come on for all the team members. Together we had created a future state where a pacemaker could produce a variety of products at the pull of the customer. (See p. 165; for a larger version see the accompanying CD.) This included:

- ❏ A pacemaker with flexible takt times to accommodate changes in customer demand
- ❏ A finished-goods supermarket that changes based on signals
- ❏ Various modes of operation throughout the year for meeting seasonal trends in customer demand

This is a real-life future state to the management team, not just another plan based on someone's idea. They liked the way that we planned to implement the system and work with operators to improve it. They also realized what this would do for their business in terms of lead-time reduction, inventory, and increased market share! The team was very excited and ready to begin implementation.

What's Next for the Team?

Many new lean concepts were covered with the team at EMC. To reinforce the learning that has taken place, we will provide an overview of how their new future state will operate in their high-mix environment. This overview will include:

- ❏ Product family demand and variation
- ❏ Receiving orders from multiple sources
- ❏ Planning and using the mix logic charts
- ❏ Scheduling the pacemaker
- ❏ Flowing the orders to shipping

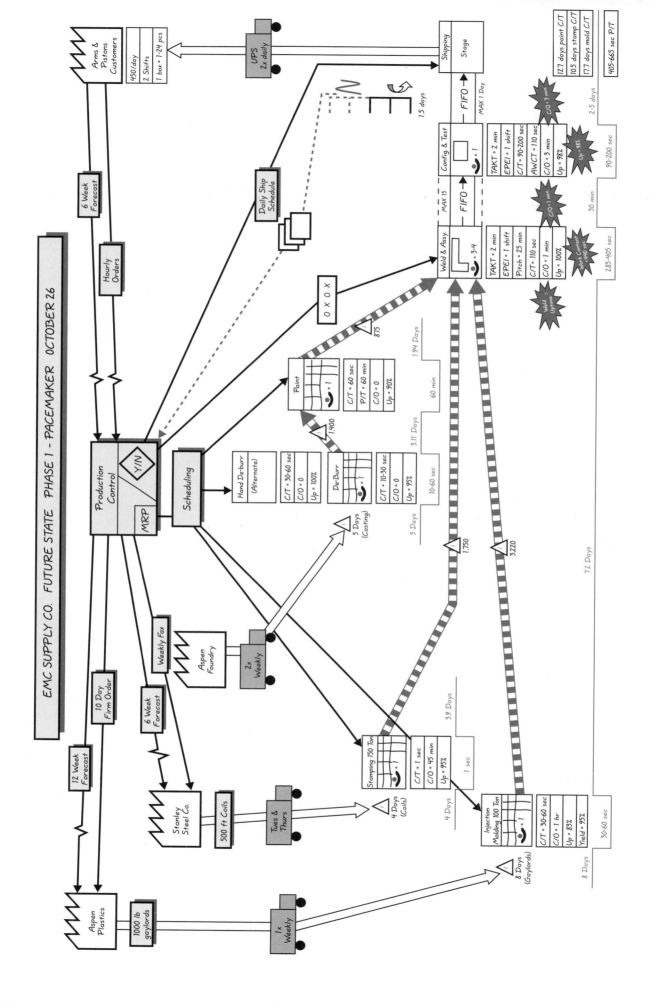

EMC SUPPLY CO. FUTURE STATE PHASE 1 - PACEMAKER OCTOBER 26

PART VI:

PUTTING IT ALL TOGETHER

❏ How Does It All Work?

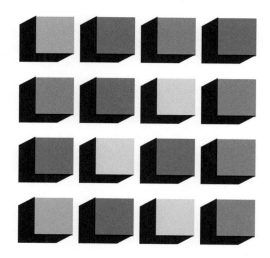

How Does It All Work?

The management team at EMC Supply was now beginning to see how they could transform their complex environment into a lean environment. They understood how to create a future-state value stream that would use the principles of flow, pull, and leveling in their mixed model environment. They also realized they had much work ahead to implement this future state. Before jumping into the implementation, we felt it best to provide an overall review of the future state in order to provide a clear understanding of its operation. So back to the whiteboard we went to put it all together for them.

First, we revised our first example (p. 25) of a make-believe product family of sensors and detectors with a new example based on actual numbers from the future-state development. The future state of the Arms & Pistons product family has a demand and variation, shown on the next page.

Prod. Code	Product Name	Anticipated Demand per Day	Range +/– %
A	Sensor-Activated Arm	65	35%
B	Laser-Activated Arm	85	50%
C	Manually Activated Arm	35	25%
D	Barcode Diverter Piston	70	10%
E	Barcode Diverter Arm	50	30%
F	Sensor-Activated Piston	55	25%
G	Laser-Activated Piston	20	10%
H	Manually Activated Piston	25	25%
X	Custom Orders	45	20%
	Total	**450**	**Max. 50%**

Next, we explained how the future state would operate with a variety of product mixes throughout the week. We explained to the management team step by step what would happen each day in their new future state.

RUNNING THE FUTURE STATE

It all starts with the customer. Customers will place orders each day, some for stock items, some for custom configurations. Orders from customers are received directly into production control via the Internet, phone, or fax. Production control knows it can produce practically any mix of products as long as the total number of products does not exceed 450 units per day. In this mix we can handle about 20 of product G, even though it exceeds takt time at the testing station. Production control takes all customer orders received, orders completed by engineering, and empty kanban cards from the supermarket (these are from products that shipped today), and they use the mix logic chart to level the mix. If a mix is exceeded, they may choose to work overtime, pull from stock, or build more of this product the next day.

Let's take an example. Say it's Monday afternoon at 4:00 P.M. All shipments for today's orders are completed at 3:30 P.M. Production control has collected the kanban cards from the shipping deck, along with all fax, phone, and Internet orders from customers.

They have also received custom orders that engineering has configured and released. The total orders for Tuesday are shown below.

Product Code	Product Name	Pack Qty.	Total Orders (pieces)	Total Orders (cases)	1st Ship Window	2nd Ship Window
			Tuesday's Orders			
A	Sensor-Activated Arm	6	48	8	4	4
B	Laser-Activated Arm	6	78	13	6	7
C	Manually Activated Arm	6	30	5	3	2
D	Barcode Diverter Piston	6	72	6	3	3
E	Barcode Diverter Arm	12	84	7	3	4
F	Sensor-Activated Piston	12	48	4	2	2
G	Laser-Activated Piston	3	27	9	5	4
H	Manually Activated Piston	3	54	18	9	9
X	Custom Orders	3	36	12	6	6
	Totals	**57**	**477**	**82**	**41**	**41**

Production control will run this mix of orders through the mix logic chart. Since the total number of units is more than 450 and the laser-activated piston is more than 20, production control will follow the mix logic chart and determine that if they build 27 of product G, they can only build 405 units of the remaining product for a total of 432 products. They will need to pull 45 units from the finished-goods supermarket or work overtime. In this case overtime would total around 90 minutes, so it would be good to pull some from finished goods.

They can now arrange the cards in the schedule box (this may be done by the material handler once the sequence rules are understood), based on ship window intervals. The cards will be arranged in each interval based on the number of operators at the pacemaker. Products G and D are placed first, as they require more operators. This will also allow the FIFO lane before the tester to accumulate a product or two when the shift starts, as product G has a long test cycle. We need these pieces there quickly because testing will also finish before takt on some products and we must have units available to make up the lost time from product G.

The beginning of the next day, the material handlers will begin their 6:00 A.M. run along their preset paths. This includes a stop at the schedule box to pick up the orders needed for the first pitch interval. They will drop the cards off at the pacemaker (welding and assembly), and continue their run. At 6:25 A.M., they will begin their next run. They will again stop by the schedule box and pick up the next pitch increment of work. They will bring this to the pacemaker and move the work completed during the first pitch increment into the FIFO lane. They may also transport the completed units from the FIFO lane following the tester to the shipping department.

The shipping department will receive a daily ship list from production control. They will place the required product on the truck from the FIFO lanes. When they do this, they will remove the kanban cards and place them in a kanban post (storage container). At the end of the day, production control will collect the cards from the kanban post and begin to arrange tomorrow's orders, along with the other orders received.

This process will repeat each day. The focus will be to build product to order and then uphold and use the necessary quantity in the supermarket to assist in leveling the schedule.

We continued to progress with the management team by reviewing the orders for the rest of the week. They noted that on Wednesday there was another problem with the mix. We asked what could be done in this case. We were pleased when they used the mix logic chart to determine the mix that could be made.

WHAT'S NEXT FOR THE TEAM?

We have now completed our future state for the pacemaker loop. This is a good start to create flow for mixed model production and eliminate waste. We may consider this phase I of the value stream as we have not addressed shared resources and suppliers.

The next step is to create an implementation plan using implementation loops[1] and measurable goals. Creating this plan can be done with any common project management tool. The ini-

---

1. For more information on implementation loops and implementation plans, refer to *Learning to See*, Mike Rother and John Shook, referenced in "Important Sources" on p. 189.

tial focus of the plan will be the pacemaker loop. For now, the team will have to schedule the upstream shared equipment in order to supply the mixed model pacemaker with the high mix of parts it can cycle through each day. After they have obtained their future state in the pacemaker loop, they will look to link in the shared resources with flow or pull, and reduce the scheduling to only one point in the value stream.

It is important to use the continuous improvement burst that we have listed in the future state as the tasks to be accomplished. We remind the team that phase I of the project should be done in no more than three to four months. After this amount of time, projects tend to fade as other projects come in. Once they have developed their plan it should be reviewed on a regular "pitch" increment. A good target for this is about every two weeks. It should also be reviewed with the most important managerial person on site, as the most important item in any factory is its future.

We will leave the team to create their plan and implement their future state at the pacemaker. After they have implemented the future state from the pacemaker towards the customer, the next steps for the team are to begin working on the next loops—shared resources and suppliers. (See p. 174; a larger version can be found on the accompanying CD.) For now, EMC management has enough to get them going to implement flow, scheduling, and leveling. So we will leave them to their tasks and wish them well, as their lean journey begins . . .

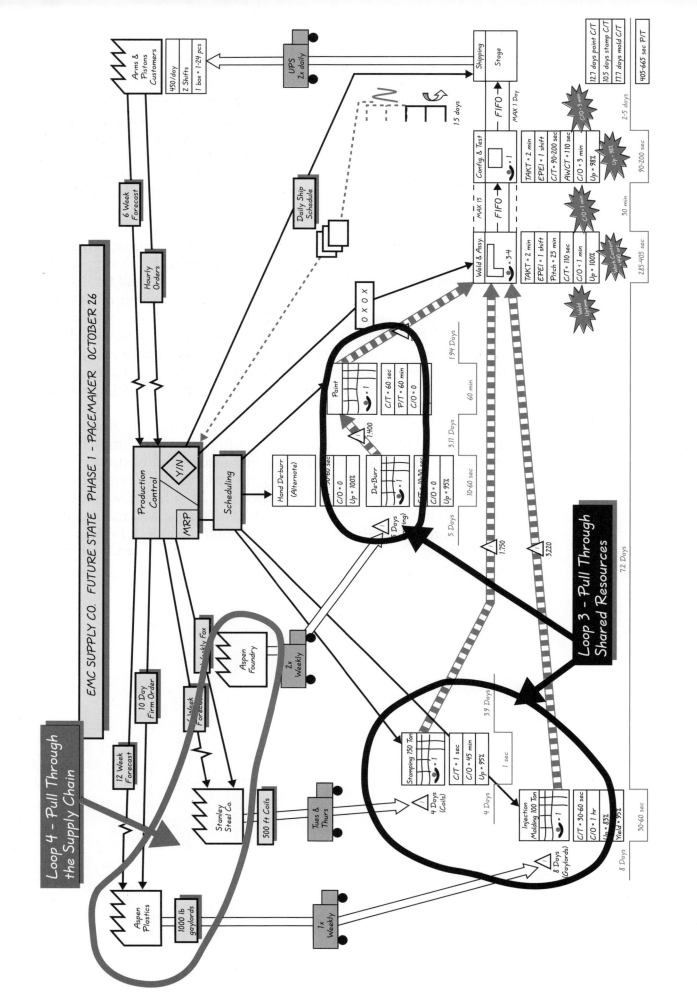

EMC SUPPLY CO. FUTURE STATE PHASE 1 - PACEMAKER OCTOBER 26

APPENDICES

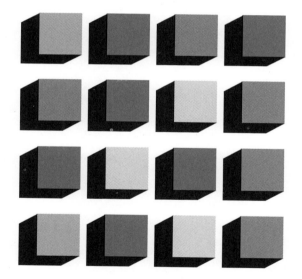

APPENDIX A:
Lean Glossary

The following glossary is a courtesy of the Lean Enterprise Institute, Canada.

Andon Board   A visual control device in a production area, typically a lighted overhead display, giving the current status of the production system and alerting team members to emerging problems.

Autonomation   Machines that are able to detect the production of a single defective part and immediately stop themselves.

Balance Chart   A bar chart that illustrates work content (by operator or workstation) and takt time. Operator balance charts are used to balance operators for flow. Machine balance charts are used to balance machines for flow.

Batch-and-Queue   Producing more than one piece of an item and then moving those items forward in a group to the next operation before they are all actually needed there. Thus, items need to wait in a queue. Also called "Batch-and-Push." (Contrast with *Continuous Flow Production*.)

Bottleneck   A process that cannot meet takt time.

Cell

A group of workstations or machines operating in a true continuous flow fashion. Work flow is linked so if work stops on one station, all work will stop in the cell. One piece flow is the best (the one with the least amount of waste) type of cell. Usually in a cell machines and workstations are placed close together in the order of processing, sometimes in a U shape. Cell operators may handle multiple processes, and the number of operators is changed when customer demand rate changes. The U-shaped equipment layout is used to allow more alternatives for distributing work elements among operators and to permit the leadoff and final operations to be performed by the same operator.

Changeover

When a piece of equipment has to stop producing in order to be fitted for producing a different item. For example, the installation of a different processing tool in a metal-working machine, a different color paint in a painting system, a new plastic resin and mold in an injection molding machine, loading different software, and so on. Changeover time is measured from the last good piece of the first product until the first good piece of the second product is produced.

Continuous Flow Production

Items are produced and moved from one processing step to the next, one piece at a time. Each process makes only the one piece that the next process needs, and the transfer batch size is one. Also called "single-piece flow" or "one-piece flow." (Contrast with *Batch-and-Queue*.)

Cycle Time

How frequently an item or product actually is completed by a process, as timed by direct observation. Also, the time it takes an operator to go through all of his or her work elements before repeating them.

Dedicated Resources

Machines or equipment that can be isolated and used solely for the purpose of building specific products or product families. They are usually low-cost equipment such as assembly stations and small presses

EPEI

Refers to "every product every interval," which is a measure of production batch size. For example, if a machine is able to changeover and produce the required quantity of all the high-running part types dedicated to it within three days, then the production batch size for each individual part type is about three days' worth of parts. Thus, this machine is making every part every three days.

Fabrication Processes	Segments of the value stream that respond to requirements from internal customers. Fabrication processes are often characterized by general-purpose equipment that changes over to make a variety of components for different downstream processes. (Compare to *Pacemaker Process*.)
FIFO	Stands for "first-in, first-out" meaning that material produced by one process is used up in the same order by the next process. FIFO is one way to regulate a queue between two decoupled processes when a supermarket or continuous flow are impractical. A FIFO queue is filled by the supplying process and emptied by the customer process. When a FIFO queue gets full, the supplying process must stop producing until the customer process has used up some of the inventory.
Five S	Five terms beginning with "S," utilized to create a workplace suited for visual control and lean production. "Sort" means to separate needed tools, parts, and instructions from unneeded materials, and to remove the latter. "Set in order" means to neatly arrange and identify parts and tools for ease of use. "Shine" means to conduct a cleanup campaign. "Standardize" means to conduct the first three S's at frequent—indeed daily—intervals to maintain a workplace in perfect condition. "Sustain" means to form the habit of always following the first four S's.
Flow	A main objective of the entire lean production effort, and one of the key concepts that passed directly from Henry Ford to Taiichi Ohno (Toyota's production manager after WWII). Ford recognized that, ideally, production should flow continuously all the way from raw material to the customer and envisioned realizing that ideal through a production system that acted as one long conveyor.
Heijunka (Load Leveling)	The act of leveling the mix and/or volume of items produced at a process over a period of time. Used to avoid excessive batching of product types and/or volume fluctuations, especially at a pacemaker process.
Information Flow	Data that tells a process what to do or produce.
Interval	The length of time it takes to cycle through all of the products within a product family. This is also a measure of flexibility and lot size (see *EPEI*).
Just-in-Time	Producing or conveying only the items that are needed by the next process, when they are needed and in the quantity needed.

Kaizen	Continuously improving in incremental steps.
Kanban	A signaling device that gives instruction for production or conveyance of items in a pull system. Can also be used to perform kaizen by reducing the number of kanban in circulation, which highlights line problems.
Lead Time	The time required for one piece to move all the way through a process or value stream, from start to finish. Envision timing a marked item as it moves from beginning to end.
Leveling	The process of filtering or smoothing customer demand to fit within the limits of the mixed model value stream.
Manufacturing Resource Planning (MRP II)	Expands MRP to include capacity planning, a finance interface to translate operations planning into financial terms and a simulation tool to assess alternative production plans. See *Material Requirements Planning (MRP)*
Material Flow	Movement of physical product through the value stream.
Material Handlers	Production-support persons who travel repeatedly along scheduled routes within a facility to transfer materials, supplies, and parts in response to pull signals and to make paced withdrawal of finished goods at pacemaker processes.
Material Requirements Planning (MRP)	A computerized system typically used to determine the quantity and timing requirements for delivery and production of items. Using MRP specifically to schedule production at processes in a value stream results in push production, because any predetermined schedule is only an estimate of what the next process will actually need. See *Manufacturing Resource Planning (MRP II)*.
Milk Run	Routing a delivery vehicle in a way that allows it to make pickups or drop-offs at multiple locations on a single travel loop, as opposed to making separate trips to each location.
Mix Logic Charts	A series of yes/no questions that lead through the process of leveling customer demand.
Mixed Model	Producing a variety or mix of products or product variations through the same value stream at the pull of the customer. Building and delivering the right quantity of a specific product (out of a high number of products available) when the customer wants it.

Monument	Any design, scheduling, or production equipment with scale requirements necessitating that designs, order, and products be brought to the machines to wait in a queue for processing. (ex. Equipment that cannot be moved as it sunk into the building.)
Operation	An activity or activities performed on a product by a single machine. (Contrast with *Process*.)
Operator Balance Chart	A bar graph depicting the cycle times of each operator in a process to make one piece compared to takt time. Useful tool for cell balancing and creating continuous flow.
Overproduction	Producing more, sooner, or faster than is required by the next process.
Paced Withdrawal	A timed sequence of withdrawal of finished product from the pacemaker process. Paced withdrawal is a method to create pitch at the pacemaker process.
Pacemaker Process	A process that is dedicated to a particular product family and is the point in which we schedule the value stream. The pacemaker also responds to orders from external customers. The pacemaker is the most important process in a facility because how you operate here determines how well you can serve the customer and what the demand pattern will be like for upstream fabrication processes.
Perfection	The complete elimination of waste so that all activities along a value stream create value.
Pitch	Pitch is the management time frame. It is a measurement of takt time performance. Pitch should also represents the frequency at which you withdraw finished goods from a pacemaker process as well as the corresponding amount of schedule you release to that process. Pitch is often calculated based on the customer's ship container quantity, but can be created using other methods.
Planned Cycle	The targeted time we balance to in order to meet customer demand, usually 92 to 95 percent of takt.
Process	A series of individual operations where material is flowing in a one-piece, continuous fashion. A process can be identified where inventory stops and accumulates.

Process Kaizen   Improvements made at an individual process or in a specific area. Sometimes called "point kaizen."

Process Village   The practice of grouping machines or activities by type of operation performed; for example, grinding machines or order entry. (Contrast with *Cell*.)

Processing Time   The time a product is actually being worked on in a machine or work area.

Product Family   A group of products that go through the same or similar downstream or "assembly" steps and equipment.

Production Smoothing   See *Heijunka*.

Pull System   An alternative to scheduling individual processes, where the customer process withdraws the items it needs from a supermarket and the supplying process produces to replenish what was withdrawn. Used to avoid push. (See also *Kanban*.)

Push   Moving work or inventory to the next process whether it is needed or not.

Queue Time   The time a product spends waiting in line for the next processing step.

Right-sized Tool   A design, scheduling, or production device that can be fitted directly into the flow of products within a product family so that production no longer requires unnecessary transport and waiting. (Contrast with definition of *Monument*.)

Shared Resources   Equipment that is used to make parts for many different product families, such as stamping, injection molding, and shears that are typically in the first few processes that transform raw material.

Spaghetti Chart   A map of the path taken by a specific product as it travels down the value stream in a mass-production organization, so-called because the product's route typically looks like a plate of spaghetti.

SPC   Statistical process control—a method whereby data is collected and statistics used to understand process stability.

Standard Work   A precise description of each work activity specifying cycle time, takt time, the work sequence of specific tasks, and the minimum inventory of parts on hand needed to conduct the activity. Any operator following this description of elements should be able to complete the work needed in the same amount of time.

Supermarket   A controlled inventory of items that is used to schedule production at an upstream process.

System Kaizen   Improvement aimed at an entire value stream.

Takt Image   Management time frame (also see *Pitch*). It is a measure of how well a plant is performing to takt.

Takt Time   The rate of customer demand; how often the customer requires one finished item. Takt time is used to design assembly and pacemaker processes, assess production conditions, calculate pitch, develop material-handling containerization and routes, determine problem-response requirements, and so on. Takt is the heartbeat of a lean system.

     Takt time is calculated by dividing production time by the quantity the customer requires in that time.

Total Productive Maintenance (TPM)   A series of methods originally pioneered by Nippondenso (a member of the Toyota group) to ensure that every machine in a production process is always able to perform its required tasks so that production is never interrupted.

Total Work Content   The amount of work that is in a product, as if one operator had built the complete product.

Value   A product's or service's capability provided to a customer at the right time at an appropriate price, as defined in each case by the customer.

Value-Added Time   Time for those work elements that transform the product in a way for which the customer is willing to pay.

Value Stream   All activities, both value-added and non-value-added, required to bring a product from raw material into the hands of the customer, a customer requirement from order to delivery, and a design from concept to launch. Value stream improvement usually begins at the door-to-door level within a facility and then expands outward to eventually encompass the full value stream.

Value Stream Loops

Segments of a value stream whose boundaries are typically marked by supermarkets. Breaking a value stream into loops is a way to divide future-state implementation into manageable pieces.

Value Stream Manager

Person responsible for creating a future-state map and leading door-to-door implementation of the future state for a particular product family. Makes change happen across departmental and functional boundaries.

Value Stream Mapping

A pencil-and-paper tool used in two stages:
a) Follow a product's production path from beginning to end and draw a visual representation of every process in the material and information flows.

b) Draw a future-state map of how value should flow. The most important map is the future-state map.

Visual Control

The placement in plain view of all tools, parts, production activities, and indicators of production system performance so that everyone involved can understand the status of the system at a glance.

Waste

Any activity that consumes resources, but creates no value for the customer.

Water Spider

See *Material Handlers*.

Work Content

How much work is required (at a station or by operator) in order to build the product. (See also *Total Work Content*.)

WIP

Stands for "work-in-process," any inventory between raw material and finished goods.

APPENDIX B:
EMC Supply Data Set

CURRENT STATE DATA SET

Sensor–Activated Arm (Part A)

Work Content Times:

Weld.	45 sec.	Paint	60 sec.
Mechanical Assy.	90 sec.	Final Assy.	130 sec.
Electrical Assy.	140 sec.	Deburr	10 sec.
		(or Hand Deburr)	30 sec.
Configure & Test	110 sec., C/O = 4 min.		

Laser–Activated Arm (Part B)

Work Content Times:

Weld.	30 sec.	Paint	60 sec.
Mechanical Assy.	60 sec.	Final Assy.	100 sec.
Electrical Assy.	140 sec.	Hand Deburr	30 sec.
Configure & Test	110 sec., C/O = 3 min.		

Manually Activated Arm (Part C)

Work Content Times:

Weld.	40 sec.	Paint	60 sec.
Mechanical Assy.	120 sec.	Final Assy.	90 sec.
Electrical Assy.	150 sec.	Deburr	20 sec.
		(or Hand Deburr)	45 sec.
Configure & Test	100 sec., C/O = 5 min.		

Barcode Diverter Piston (Part D)

Work Content Times:

Weld.	35 sec.	Paint	60 sec.
Mechanical Assy.	90 sec.	Final Assy.	140 sec.
Electrical Assy.	180 sec.	Deburr	15 sec.
		(or Hand Deburr)	30 sec.
Configure & Test	110 sec., C/O = 5 min.		

Barcode Diverter Arm (Part E)

Work Content Times:

Weld.	45 sec.	Paint	60 sec.
Mechanical Assy.	100 sec.	Final Assy.	105 sec.
Electrical Assy.	180 sec.	Deburr	30 sec.
		(or Hand Deburr)	60 sec.
Configure & Test	105 sec., C/O = 3 min.		

Sensor-Activated Piston (Part F)

Work Content Times:

Weld.	40 sec.	Paint	60 sec.
Mechanical Assy.	85 sec.	Final Assy.	90 sec.
Electrical Assy.	105 sec.	Deburr	10 sec.
		(or Hand Deburr)	30 sec.
Configure & Test	90 sec., C/O = 5 min.		

Laser-Activated Piston (Part G)

Work Content Times:

Weld.	35 sec.	Paint	60 sec.
Mechanical Assy.	150 sec.	Final Assy.	140 sec.
Electrical Assy.	130 sec.	Hand Deburr	30 sec.
Configure & Test	200 sec., C/O = 5 min.		

Manually Activated Piston (Part H)

Work Content Times:

Weld.	35 sec.	Paint	60 sec.
Mechanical Assy.	80 sec.	Final Assy.	100 sec.
Electrical Assy.	145 sec.	Deburr	10 sec.
		(or Hand Deburr)	30 sec.
Configure & Test	100 sec., C/O = 4 min.		

FUTURE STATE DATA SET

Sensor-Activated Arm (Part A)

Work Content Times:

Weld.	35 sec.	Paint	60 sec.
Mechanical Assy.	75 sec.	Final Assy.	100 sec.
Electrical Assy.	110 sec.	Deburr	10 sec.
		(or Hand Deburr)	30 sec.
Configure & Test	110 sec., C/O = 2 min.		

Laser-Activated Arm (Part B)

Work Content Times:

Weld.	25 sec.	Paint	60 sec.
Mechanical Assy.	50 sec.	Final Assy.	90 sec.
Electrical Assy.	120 sec.	Hand Deburr	30 sec.
Configure & Test	110 sec., C/O = 2 min.		

Manually Activated Arm (Part C)

Work Content Times:

Weld.	30 sec.	Paint	60 sec.
Mechanical Assy.	100 sec.	Final Assy.	85 sec.
Electrical Assy.	110 sec.	Deburr	20 sec.
		(or Hand Deburr)	45 sec.
Configure & Test	100 sec., C/O = 2 min.		

Barcode Diverter Piston (Part D)

Work Content Times:

Weld.	30 sec.	Paint	60 sec.
Mechanical Assy.	90 sec.	Final Assy.	125 sec.
Electrical Assy.	160 sec.	Deburr	15 sec.
		(or Hand Deburr)	30 sec.
Configure & Test	110 sec., C/O = 3 min.		

Barcode Diverter Arm (Part E)

Work Content Times:

Weld.	40 sec.	Paint	60 sec.
Mechanical Assy.	75 sec.	Final Assy.	75 sec.
Electrical Assy.	140 sec.	Deburr	30 sec.
		(or Hand Deburr)	60 sec.
Configure & Test	105 sec., C/O = 2 min.		

Sensor-Activated Piston (Part F)

Work Content Times:

Weld.	35 sec.	Paint	60 sec.
Mechanical Assy.	80 sec.	Final Assy.	85 sec.
Electrical Assy.	120 sec.	Deburr	10 sec.
		(or Hand Deburr)	30 sec.
Configure & Test	90 sec., C/O = 2 min.		

Laser-Activated Piston (Part G)

Work Content Times:

Weld.	30 sec.	Paint	60 sec.
Mechanical Assy.	135 sec.	Final Assy.	140 sec.
Electrical Assy.	130 sec.	Hand Deburr	30 sec.
Configure & Test	200 sec., C/O = 2 min.		

Manually Activated Piston (Part H)

Work Content Times:

Weld.	30 sec.	Paint	60 sec.
Mechanical Assy.	70 sec.	Final Assy.	95 sec.
Electrical Assy.	125 sec.	Deburr	10 sec.
		(or Hand Deburr)	30 sec.
Configure & Test	100 sec., C/O = 4 min.		

Important Sources

Some of the concepts used in this book are based upon previous books on value stream mapping and cell design. These books are fundamental in implementing lean. I would like to acknowledge these works as references for this book and encourage readers to also review these texts to assist them in their lean journeys.

Lean Thinking—James P. Womack and Daniel T. Jones., Simon & Schuster, 1996.

Learning to See—Mike Rother and John Shook. The Lean Enterprise Institute, 1998.

Learning to See, Version 1.2—Mike Rother and John Shook. The Lean Enterprise Institute, 1999.

Creating Continuous Flow—Mike Rother and Rick Harris. The Lean Enterprise Institute, 2001.

FOR FURTHER READING

Becoming Lean—Jeffrey K. Liker (ed.). Productivity Press, 1998.

Reorganizing the Factory: Competing through Cellular Manufacturing—Nancy Hyer and Urban Wemmerlöv. Productivity Press, 2002.

Value Stream Management—Eight Steps to Planning, Mapping, and Sustaining Lean Improvements—Don Tapping and Tom Shuker. Productivity Press, 2002.

Kanban for the Shopfloor—The Productivity Press Development Team. Productivity Press, 2002.

Kaizen for the Shopfloor—The Productivity Press Development Team. Productivity Press, 2002.

Pull Production for the Shopfloor—The Productivity Press Development Team. Productivity Press, 1998.

Quick Response Manufacturing—Rajan Suri. Productivity Press, 1998.

Time Based Manufacturing—Joseph A. Bockerstette and Richard L. Shell. Institute of Industrial Engineers and McGraw-Hill, 1993.

Index

About the Author

Kevin J. Duggan, President, Duggan and Associates, Inc., a lean advisory firm specializing in teaching companies from small start-ups through Fortune 100 how to become lean, is also a faculty member of the Lean Enterprise Institute and the Lean Enterprise Institute Canada.

Kevin's lean knowledge comes from developing and implementing lean concepts in the early 90's. In the midst of batch manufacturing, Kevin was able to develop and pioneer lean concepts into the world's largest toy company, where he rose through various management positions to eventually become Corporate Director of Operations Engineering. There he developed advanced concepts of flow and mixed model and implemented these throughout many companies across North America. In 1999 Kevin began working with the Lean Enterprise Institute as a faculty member and also as a Director for the Lean Enterprise Institute Canada while he continued to mentor companies implementing lean. Kevin received a B.S. in Mechanical Engineering from Roger Williams College in Rhode Island.

Kevin has many worked with many executives and taught many companies how to implement lean thinking into their organization. These include major companies such as Whirlpool, General Mills, Perkin Elmer, Gorton's, Sikorsky Aircraft, Georgia Pacific, United Technologies, Messier-Dowty, Thomas & Betts, Indalex, Tecomet-Viasys, and many others. His work has spanned a variety of industries such as aerospace, medical, high tech, machine shops, extrusion, consumer products, and other industries.

He also developed numerous workshops including the Mixed Model Value Streams that have been taught for the Lean Enterprise Institute and the Lean Enterprise Institute Canada.

Kevin believes that the successful lean journey is accomplished through teaching. His natural ability to teach others practical, hands on techniques for applying lean (even in complex environments) has enable companies to transform their culture.

KEVIN ON LEAN:

"The most successful Lean Transformation occurs when learning and understanding take place through problem solving and process improvement at all levels. It's not just an engineer's responsibility to see waste in a lean environment; every employee must learn to see it before it can be eliminated."

"Many companies apply lean tools with the goal of increased productivity; they attempt to reach a targeted number for improvement, believing lean will help them obtain their management objectives. The focus then becomes internal rather than on the customer, and Lean is relegated to 'flavor of the month' status with no long-term, sustained transformation achieved. Lean consists of many tools, some very advanced, and applying these tools does not necessarily equal transformation; changing the company's culture does."

To find out more about Kevin and his company, visit *www.dugganinc.com*.